The similarity of the elemental circumstances leaves no doubt but that all the murders were committed by the same person and that there is some eccentric motive for his crimes.
Beaumont Enterprise, 1912

Other Books in the Dead Men Do Tell Tales Series by Troy Taylor

VICTIMS OF THE AX FIEND

MYSTERY, MAYHEM AND THE CHURCH OF SACRIFICE MURDERS

TROY TAYLOR

AN AMERICAN HAUNTINGS INK BOOK

Original Cover Artwork Designed by
© Copyright 2020 by April Slaughter & Troy Taylor

This Book is Published By:
American Hauntings Ink
Jacksonville, Illinois | 217.791.7859
Visit us on the Internet at
http://www.americanhauntingsink.com

First Edition – May 2020
ISBN: 978-1-7324079-9-2

Printed in the United States of America

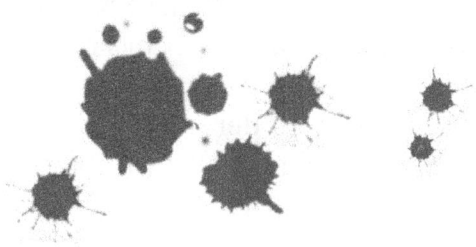

It started with a telephone call.

Honestly, it started before that, but it was a telephone call in January 1911 that gave the first indication to the police that they were not dealing with a handful of random killings. Most of the ax murders that occurred in Louisiana and Texas during that a three-year period were the work of a single killer - a "repeat murderer" as they called serial killers at a time when that term didn't yet exist - and he was not finished with his bloody business.

The first hint of what some called the "Church of Sacrifice Murders" came to the attention of the authorities when a police officer in West Crowley, Louisiana, took an urgent call from neighbors who feared that something terrible had happened at 605 Western Avenue. When Officer Bellew arrived at the house, he found that the home's three occupants - a man, a woman, and a young boy - had been murdered in their beds. Their skulls had been split open. The mattresses were soaked with blood, and smeared footprints were on the floor. The doors were all bolted from the inside, suggesting that the killer had entered the house through a window and killed everyone while they slept. In the corner of one room was a basin filled with bloody water. Propped against the foot of a bed was the murder weapon - a blood-stained ax.

A local newspaper called the crime "the most brutal murder in the history of this section," but it would turn out to be one of many ax slayings across Louisiana and Texas in the early 1910s. Over time, newspapers would "reveal" that the murders were connected to a deranged Voodoo cult called the "Church of the Sacrifice," which claimed its victims for bloody rituals.

Well, some of them might have been.

Let me clarify that -- they might have been if the so-called "Voodoo cult" actually existed. You see, nothing was what it seemed in Louisiana and Texas between 1909 and 1912. There were the alleged cult murders, and then there was something perhaps even more sinister - the lone killer who was preying on poor families in the deep South.

The Axman -- as most would later call him - was no worshipper of the supernatural. He was one of the most prolific killers in American history, rivaling even the infamous "Billy the Axman," who would claim victims across the Midwest, including the Moore family in Villisca, Iowa, around this same time.

The killers in Louisiana and Texas would eventually claim at least 45 men, women, and children, from 12 families across the Deep South. These horrendous crimes not only remain unsolved, but they are largely unknown more than a century later.

Why? Why is this story not as famous as the stories of the murders that occurred in Villisca and across the Midwest? They are eerily similar in that the killer was never caught, he left gruesome crime scenes behind, and even likely traveled by train from town to town.

The answer to that is both tragic and regrettable - all the victims of the Axman in Louisiana and Texas were black.

The only exception was the white wife of a black man in San Antonio, but that did not keep her from being killed along with her husband and three children.

The murders created a tremendous amount of panic among the African American communities of Texas and Louisiana between 1909 and 1912. It was a widespread fear that one's entire family might be wiped out ruthlessly while they were sleeping. The terror, as it turned out, was well-justified. Dozens of people lost their lives. The panic was surprisingly well-documented by the press at the time, mostly thanks to the sensational nature of the killings and the lurid tales of black magic and Voodoo that later surrounded them. Another name given to the murders also hints at why these murders have been largely forgotten - the "Mulatto Ax Murders."

The murders remain unsolved to this day. Although suspects were speculated about - and some even arrested - no definite conclusion about the killer's identity was ever reached. Some have blamed the failure to find the killer on the fact that the police didn't bother to work as hard as they would have if the victims had been white. That is a distinct possibility, especially based on the location and the time period, but as the reader will discover, many of the officers in charge of the various investigations did all they could to find the perpetrators. They were simply unmatched by the deviousness of the Axman and hamstrung by the shortcomings of forensic detection at the time.

Many are surprised to learn that it was not the police who were overtly racist about the crimes, it was the newspapers. The way that the white press looked at these murders provides an often-disturbing insight into the distance that the white community felt toward the black community during the days of Jim Crow. The murders were even used to terrorize black individuals and communities with letters threatening attacks by the Axman. It became clear in the press accounts that the panic among African Americans in the region lasted long after the killings came to an end - and that much of the panic was created by the newspapers themselves.

There is no question, though, that black families had every reason to be afraid.

None of them were prepared for a killer like this. The Axman didn't just kill one person - he wiped out entire families. He came in the night and he vanished without ever being seen. His victims were always poor, so robbery was never the motive, and he usually left the murder weapon behind at the scene of the crime. Each of the crime scenes was always a stone's throw away from the tracks of the Southern Pacific Railroad, suggesting that he had arrived by train and left town the same way.

Small towns became terrifying places. The fear felt by black families became a paranoia that permeated the entire town. No one slept well at night - out of fear of the killer and because of fear of being shot by those who stood guard against the Axman. To make things worse each of the murders was followed by the arrival of "hoodoo doctors" who came to town selling charms to keep away the killer. But would they work? Most feared they wouldn't because rumors had spread that the Axman had Voodoo talismans of his own, which was how he avoided detection.

And perhaps his gris-gris bags worked because the Axman was never found. He took the secrets of his killings with him to the grave. The Axman vanished in the spring of 1912 and he was never heard from again, leaving a legacy of terror and mystery in his wake.

The strange story of this Axman is not only uniquely Southern - but it's uniquely American, too. It's a snapshot of a time and place that is thankfully long past, and yet it still reverberates today. It's a story of crime, murder, mystery, black magic, Voodoo, and the racism that runs through every part of it.

It's also a story that just might convince you to leave the lights burning when you are home with your family at night. I've been waiting many years to properly tell this tale, so I hope the wait was worth it.

And that it makes it apparent that the murders in Iowa - and elsewhere in the Midwest around this time - were not the only massacres that occurred in America during what most considered the "good ol' days."

Troy Taylor
Spring 2020

I. "THE BLUNT END OF AN AX WAS USED"

SAN ANTONIO, TEXAS - MARCH 21, 1911

On the morning of March 21, 1911, Louis Casaway didn't report for work. For many people missing a day of work would not be strange, but it was for Louis. Not only was he a hard worker but he was also one of the most respected men in the community, black or white. When he didn't report to work that morning, it was obvious that something was wrong.

Alfred Louis Casaway was an African American Creole man who was born and raised in New Orleans and moved to San Antonio in 1876 or 1877. He was respected in political circles, was a member of the laborer's board, served as bailiff for grand jury hearings, and worked as a porter and messenger at City Hall before taking a job as a custodian at Grant School. He was well-known around the community, was a musician, and appeared in the local newspapers on many occasions during the time he lived in San Antonio. In 1899 he was lauded for his organization of a Juneteenth event to celebrate the end of slavery, and he was an active member of the Republican party. In 1895 his name was listed as being part of a group that thanked the mayor for taking down wanted posters of local rapists, which were creating a motive for racial violence.

Louis also had a high-profile social life. His 36th birthday made the newspapers at the top of a list of local events. In 1898 a close friend who was a famous Cuban War veteran stayed with him, earning him another mention in the papers.

Louis's wife, Elizabeth Castelow, or Lizzie, as most people knew her, was from Hallertsville, Texas, a small town about 100 miles east of San Antonio. Born in 1874, she lived with her widowed father until he remarried when Lizzie was 15. Soon after she met a young cowboy named Sam Lane and they were married. About eight months later he told her to fix supper while he rounded up a few cattle and he was never seen again. The next year she moved to San Antonio and began working as a seamstress. In this new city, she met Louis and the two of them fell in love, even though their relationship seemed doomed from the start since Lizzie was white. Any marriage between them would violate the laws against the mixing of races.

Such laws were nicknamed the "Jim Crow Laws," a name attributed to "Jump Jim Crow," a song-and-dance caricature of blacks that were performed in blackface, starting in the 1820s. Within a decade it became a pejorative expression meaning "Negro." When southern legislatures began passing laws directed against blacks in the late nineteenth century, the laws earned the racist moniker - all the way to the end of them in the 1960s.

But Jim Crow was more than just a series of rigid anti-black laws; it was a way of life for African Americans. They became second-class citizens. Many white Christian ministers taught that whites were the chosen people, blacks were cursed to be servants, and that God supported racial segregation.

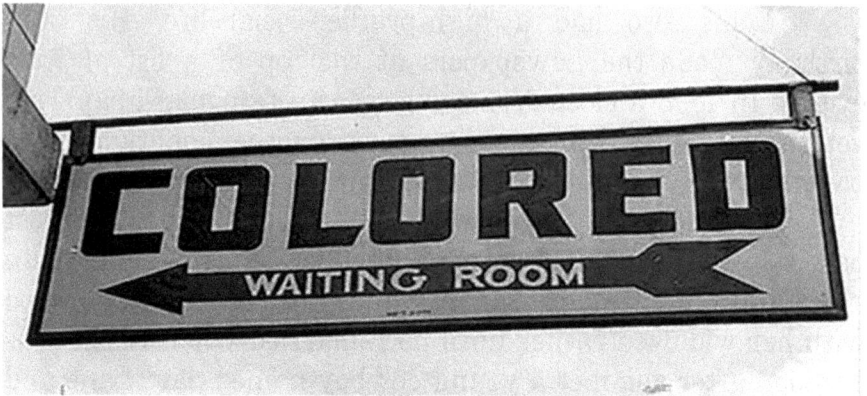

The era of Jim Crow forced African Americans into separate restrooms, swimming pools, schools, and more, all across America, but especially in the South

Teachers supported the belief that blacks were intellectually inferior to whites. Politicians gave speeches on the dangers of integration and its dangers to the white race. Newspaper and magazine writers routinely referred to African Americans as niggers, coons, and darkies. Even games played by children portrayed blacks as inferior beings. Every part of society supported the oppression of blacks during those years.

The Jim Crow system was built around the idea that whites were superior to blacks in all important ways, including intelligence, morality, and civilized behavior. For instance, a black man could not offer to shake hands with a white man because it suggested he thought he was socially equal. A black man could never offer a hand to a white woman, or he could be accused of rape.

Blacks and white were not supposed to eat together. If they had to eat together the whites were served first and some sort of partition had to be placed between the races.

Blacks were not allowed to show affection toward one another in public, especially kissing, because it offended white people. Whites never used courtesy titles of respect when referring to blacks - no Mr., Mrs., Sir, or Ma'am. Instead, they called blacks by their first names. Blacks always had to use courtesy titles when referring to whites and were never allowed to call them by their first name.

If a black person rode in a vehicle driven by a white person, the black person sat in the back seat or the back of a truck. White motorists always had the right-of-way at all intersections.

These were all forms of Jim Crow etiquette. The laws were something else altogether, excluding blacks from public transportation, from juries, certain jobs, and most neighborhoods. There had been three amendments to the Constitution passed to grant blacks the same legal protections as whites. However, after 1877, and the election of Republican Rutherford B. Hayes, almost all southern and border states began restricting the liberties of African American citizens. Things were made worse by the U.S. Supreme Court when it undermined the Constitutional protections of blacks with the infamous Plessy vs. Ferguson case in 1896, which legitimized Jim Crow laws and that way of life.

In 1890 Louisiana passed what was called the "Separate Car Law," which claimed to "aid passenger comfort" by creating "separate but equal" cars for blacks and whites. But this was a farce - no public accommodations, including railway travel, provided blacks with equal facilities. This law made it illegal for blacks to sit in seats reserved for whites. In 1891 a group of black men decided to test the Jim Crow law. Home A. Plessy - who was seven-eighths white and one-eighth black, which made him black - sat in a whites-only railroad car. He was arrested and his lawyer presented the argument that Louisiana did not have the right to label one citizen as white

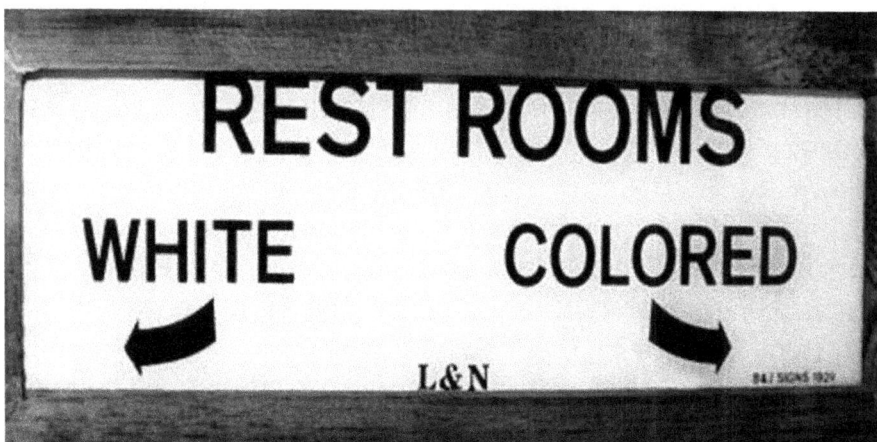

The laws and traditions of this era were supported by churches, local governments, and even teachers, who instructed their students that African Americans were inferior to whites.

and another black when attempting to restrict their rights and privileges. The case went all the way to the Supreme Court, which decided that as long as state governments provided legal access and legal freedoms for blacks, equal to those of whites, they could maintain separate institutions to make these rights available. The Court had voted 7-2 in favor of Louisiana's racist laws and legitimized two societies - one white and advantaged, and the other black, disadvantaged, and despised. The court's decision sent a message to southern states that proclaimed that discrimination against African Americans was acceptable.

Jim Crow states passed statutes that severely regulated all interaction between the races. Signs were placed at water fountains, on entrances and exit doors, and in front of public facilities. There were separate hospitals for blacks and whites, separate prisons, separate schools, separate churches, separate cemeteries, separate public restrooms, and separate public

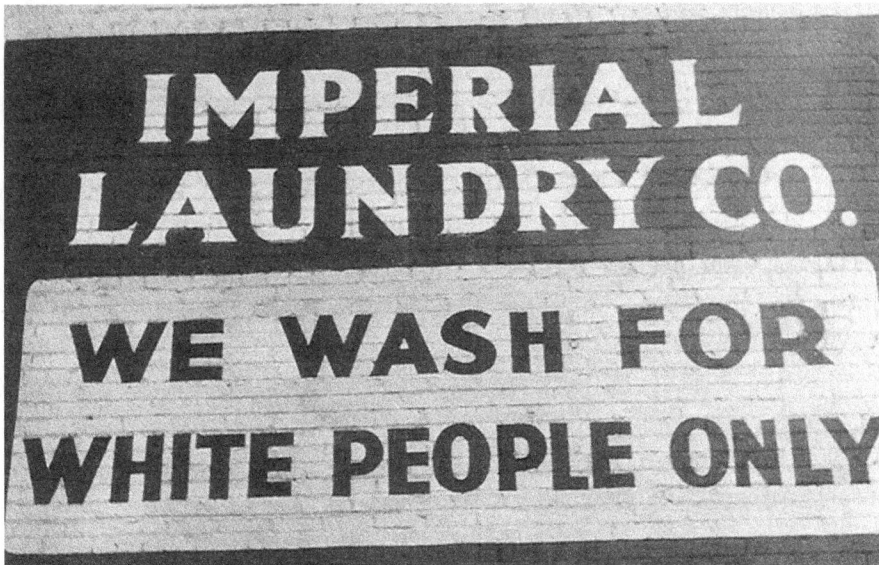

Jim Crow was a way of life – for whites and blacks alike – in the South of the late 1800s and first half of the 1900s.

accommodations. Blacks were confined to the balcony in movie theaters and made to sit in the back of the bus. In almost every case the black facilities were inferior, older, and more run-down. In other cases, there were no black facilities at all - no "Colored" restroom, no public beach, no place to sit or to eat. The Plessy case gave states a legal way to ignore their obligations to their black citizens.

Jim Crow laws touched every aspect of everyday life. Children couldn't play together in parks and could never attend school together. Black barbers couldn't cut the hair of white people. Black and white passengers had to sit in separate parts of the bus, and they couldn't even sit in the same waiting room at the station. Separate libraries were created for blacks. Prisoners had to be confined in separate jails. White liquor stores could not sell to blacks. Even the dead had to be buried in separate cemeteries.

Blacks who violated the Jim Crow laws - or even the traditions and etiquette - faced violence, both real and threatened. Blacks who drank from white water fountains or tried to vote risked their homes, their jobs, and even their lives. Whites could physically beat blacks if they felt like it. Blacks had little legal recourse against these attacks because the Jim Crow criminal justice system was all-white --- the police, prosecutors, judges, juries, and prison officials.

Violence was always lurking under the surface of Jim Crow. Blacks could be controlled that way. The most extreme forms of Jim Crow violence were lynchings.

Lynchings were public murders carried out by mobs. There were thousands of them in the late nineteenth century and early twentieth-century South. Most victims were hanged or shot, but some were burned at the stake, beaten by clubs, castrated, or dismembered. It was a way to intimidate blacks and "keep them in their places." Many whites claimed that although lynchings were distasteful, they were needed to help a justice system that was overwhelmed by blacks who were prone to violent crimes, notably the rapes of white women.

Under Jim Crow all sexual interactions between black men and white women were forbidden - they were illegal, illicit, socially repugnant, and were defined as rape by Jim Crow laws. Even though only a small percentage of lynching victims were accused of rape, lynch law was often supported on the popular belief that lynchings were necessary to protect white women from being violated by black rapists. In truth, most blacks were raped for demanding civil rights, violating Jim Crow etiquette, or in the aftermath of race riots - in the

South and the North - which led to mass lynchings and murders of African Americans.

In almost every race riot that occurred, it was white people who sparked the incident by attacking black people. Riots occurred in large cities - like Chicago, Tulsa, St. Louis, and other places - and the majority took place during the hot summer months.

Rumors always played an extremely important role in causing the riots and usually involved some alleged criminal activity by blacks against whites, leading to violence. Most often the local police force was involved as a precipitating cause or perpetuating factor in the riots. And nearly every time the police sided with the white attackers, either by participating in the riot or failing to stop it. In addition, local newspapers often published inflammatory articles about "black criminals" immediately before the riots, helping to kick things off.

It would be those riots - which saw the deaths of blacks, and their homes and businesses looted and burned - that helped to bring an end to the Jim Crow laws. In the 1930s and 1940s, black organizations like the NAACP began protesting the "separate but equal" laws in the country. In 1954, the Supreme Court overturned Plessy vs. Ferguson with Brown vs. the Board of Education. Rosa Parks refused to give up her seat on a bus to a white man, and by the middle 1960s, new laws were passed that finally made discrimination illegal - even if America had been slow to change.

But the civil rights movement, along with new and hopeful laws, were many years in the future for the poor African Americans of Texas and Louisiana in the early 1910s. It was in this era of repression and segregation that Louis

Casaway and Lizzie Castelow struggled to make a life for themselves.

The Jim Crow laws made it impossible for them to get married in Texas, so they crossed the border to Mexico, obtained a license, and got married there. When they returned to San Antonio legal proceedings were started against them and Lizzie was summoned to appear before a grand jury. Louis was so well-liked in the community that the grand jury declined to indict them.

They moved into a three-room house at 517 North Olive Street and, by all accounts, had a happy marriage. By March 1911 they had three children: Josie, age 6, Louise, age 3, and Alfred, who was five months old.

After Josie had been born in 1904 Louis cut back on his political activity, left his job at City Hall, and took a position as a custodian at Grant School, a segregated elementary school for African American children.

On Tuesday morning, March 21, students began arriving for school but found the doors were locked and they were unable to get inside. Louis had the keys. Concerned, Principal Tarver called the home of Louis's brother-in-law, Richard A. Campbell, to check on him. Louis's sister was married to Campbell, a local attorney, and the Campbells lived in a house that adjoined the Casaway home. Campbell was also Louis's landlord.

When the telephone rang at the Campbell home it was answered by a Bessie Drakes, who rented rooms from the Campbells. She had a young son who often played with the Casaway children and sometimes spent the night with them. On Monday evening Josie and Louise had been playing outside with the Drakes boy but, around sundown, Bessie went over

The Casaway home in March 1911

to the Casaway house and brought him home - a casual decision that undoubtedly saved his life.

Bessie took the call from the school and then went next door to check on the Casaways. She knocked loudly, but there was no answer. She returned to the Campbells and told Delia, Richard's wife and Louis's sister, that she couldn't get any response. Delia went next door to see for herself. She circled the house, calling to her brother and his family, and knocking on doors and windows to try and find a way in.

The house was locked up tight. The windows were mostly covered, but from what she could see it was dark inside. No one was moving around. Alarmed now, she hurried back home and got her husband.

Campbell, unable to get into the house through any of the doors, finally pried off a screen and forced open a window. When he opened it a bed pillow fell from the windowsill. It had been blocking their view of the inside of the house. With the pillow out of the way, he saw the bloody body of Louis on the bed. Horrified, he ran back immediately to his house and called the police.

As soon as news of the murder spread through the neighborhood curiosity-seekers hurried to the scene. A photographer for a local paper arrived early and captured an image of the house. By the time officers from both the police and sheriff's departments arrived the streets were blocked by a crowd of over 500 of the morbidly curious, both black and white. The number continued to grow throughout the day. Even in a town that had seen as much crime as San Antonio in years past, few had ever witnessed the brutality inside of the Casaway home.

Bexar County Sheriff John Tobin was one of the first investigators at the scene. He had a personal interest in the murders. He not only knew Louis Casaway from his work as a grand jury bailiff but also knew Lizzie, who had worked in his home as a seamstress. He liked both of them very much. Tobin immediately offered a $250 reward for any clue that led to the apprehension of the killer. He hunted down many leads in the months to come and, at times, believe he was near to solving the murders. In the end, though, he would be haunted by the case for the rest of his life.

The Casaway murders were the most horrible and brutal that had taken place in San Antonio at the time. All five had been murdered, their skulls crushed by the blunt side of an ax. The weapon had been taken from the family's own woodshed and it had been left behind at the scene, propped up at the foot of a bad. The walls of the house were spattered with blood, cast off with the swinging of the ax.

Louis was found dead in the bed where his brother-in-law had first seen him. The body of his three-year-old daughter, Louise, was next to him. Lying in a bed in an adjoining room were the bodies of Lizzie, along with six-year-old Josie and five-month-old Alfred.

When the police had arrived at the house, they found the back door had been jammed shut, not locked. The killer had apparently jammed the door, wedging something into it so that it would be difficult to open. The house had not been ransacked. Nothing was out of place. There was blood on the walls, the ceiling, the floor, and even on a child's doll, but aside from that, the house was neat and clean.

Robbery was ruled out as a motive from the start of the investigation. In Louis's trousers, found at the foot of the bed, was a gold watch, a case with an image of St. Joseph on it, and a purse with some coins in it. His pants also held a ring of 13 keys, some of which were supposed to have been used to unlock the school that morning.

None of the neighbors had heard anything out of the ordinary during the night. It had started raining on the previous evening around 11:00 p.m., and yet the police found no sign of mud or water that had been tracked into the house - just footprints leading away from the back door. They believed that the killer must have entered the house before the rain started - and possibly hid inside, unknown to the family - and only left after the killing was finished.

A local newspaper, the *San Antonio Light and Gazette*, described the scene:

That the person who committed the crime was deliberate in his work of slaughter is shown by the condition of things found upon the arrival of the officers. The faces of Louis Casaway and his wife were found covered with a cloth. In the window near which Louis Casaway lay, a pillow had been placed. A pillow was also found in the window near the

Clipped from the *San Antonio Express* story about the Casaway murders

head of the woman and a blanket had been spread across the north window of this room.

Josie Casaway was killed while lying on the bed nearest the wall of the north room, as shown by the blood at that spot. The body, however, had been picked up and afterwards thrown near the foot of the bed, the head being bent farther back than was the larger portion of the body. Other conditions found in the room indicated that the murderer was in no hurry to leave. In each killing, the blunt end of the ax had been used.

The lack of useful clues didn't prevent the sheriff's department from making a few arrests. That night a black suspect was arrested, largely because he'd had a disagreement with Louis at some point in the past and the other man had threatened his life. His feet were also about the right size to fit the footprints in the mud. Nothing tied him to the crime, though, and he was released the following day.

Officers returned to the scene of the crime and carefully examined every piece of clothing and item of furniture in the house. They pored over the walls and floors, looking for any kind of clue. Unfortunately, their crude forensic examination yielded no clues for the untrained investigators.

Once again, a large crowd of onlookers of all races gathered in the street. They placed boxes and benches under the windows so that they could more easily peer inside. The bloody mattresses, sheets, and clothing were placed in the front yard, scheduled to be burned. A newspaper reporter noted that "several negroes protested they should be buried, because they were covered with human blood."

Arrangements for the burial of the family were handled by the Williamson and St. Clair Funeral Parlor. Ironically, one of the owners, Perry Sinclair (St. Clair apparently sounded more religious for advertising purposes), was the son-in-law of Richard Campbell, Louis's brother-in-law. The funeral services were held at St. Paul's Methodist Church and the bodies were interred at City Cemetery No. 3. Three caskets were used - one for Louis, one for Lizzie and little Alfred, and Josie and Louise in the third. Newspapers noted that the services were "attended by nearly all the negroes living near where the Casaways had lived. The murders and the funeral were the sole topics of conversation, almost, yesterday along North Olive Street between East Commerce and Nolan Streets, and many of the negroes were wrought up to a high pitch."

Once the bodies were placed in their graves and night began to fall over the neighborhood the crowds that had surrounded the Casaway house faded away. According to the

San Antonio Express, many of the people who lived in the neighborhood quickly came to believe the house was haunted.

Faces pressed to windows and peered around corners to watch over the house at night. The Casaway family's dog - the only survivor of the massacre - refused to leave the front doorstep. A reporter for the newspaper wrote:

About 11 o'clock, close to the hour at which the murders are believed to have been committed, a little party of negroes was seated in a house nearby. The dog, which had been quiet for some time, suddenly began howling again, attracting attention to it. As the persons in the group looked that way a blue light appeared suddenly to leap from the windows of the house. It vanished, but a moment later again shone forth. Looking closer, it appeared to the frightened watchers that a light shone dimly in the house. One of the party was sure he heard the sound of a blow, followed by a sharp cry. The report spread quickly, and soon many eyes were focused on the house. For thirty minutes the blue light appeared to shine and then went out altogether. What caused it, whether a reflection from a distant electric light or what, is not known. No investigation was made. No one cared to approach the house.

As the investigation grew increasingly colder, a failure to find new clues led to speculation. It was suggested that the Casaways had been drugged, which was how family members had been murdered in separate rooms without waking anyone in the opposite room. However, detectives decided not to have the contents of their stomachs examined, feeling that they had other clues that would lead them to the killer, or killers.

If the family was drugged perhaps their dog had also been drugged. This was a suggestion to explain why the family pet had not barked or alerted the Casaways to a trespasser. This led to speculation that perhaps the dog had known the identity of the killer. Perhaps the animal was familiar enough with that person not to bark when the murderer entered the house. The Casaways had owned the dog for a year and it had been kept on the back porch - the way the killer had exited the house - but it had never barked.

Other detectives, as well as Sheriff Tobin, believed that it had been a racial murder -- someone was driven mad by the fact that Louis was black, and Elizabeth was white. Even though Louis was well-liked and his neighbors, as well as other people in town, remained accepting of the marriage, the racial issue could not be ignored.

And it would continue to be raised, especially when other murders across Texas and Louisiana began to be connected to the murders of the Casaways. In all those cases the victims were predominately mulattoes.

It seemed difficult to believe that someone would be deranged enough to kill a man, woman, and three small children with an ax over the color of their skin, but it had happened. This wasn't the first of the Axman's murders - and it wouldn't be the last.

After more than a week had passed the murders caught the attention of other Texas newspapers, as well as in Louisiana, New Mexico, Oklahoma, Kansas, California, Utah, and Illinois. Faced with increasing pressure for a killing that was described as "the most remarkable in the criminal annals of Texas," the murderer leaving absolutely no clue to his or her identity, Texas Governor Branch Colquitt offered a $250 reward for the killer of the Casaways. Two days later the concerned black community of San Antonio held a meeting to raise more money for the reward fund. A grand jury was empaneled by Judge Edward Dwyer to investigate the murders, but with no suspects, they had no one to indict.

Meanwhile, Sheriff Tobin had been searching for Lizzie's family members. Two brothers were located - one in Llano and one in Austin - and both were questioned by a deputy sheriff and as city detective, but neither was able to offer any information that helped the investigation. Several of Lizzie's relatives, including her brother, John, the cattleman from Llano, were eventually called before the grand jury. Most of them had assumed that Lizzie was dead long before she was murdered. The family had largely written her off after she had married a black man.

But it was a more distant relative who had not been interviewed that was arrested for the murders four months later after he had been tricked into showing up at the sheriff's office.

William McWilliams was a 68-year-old man who had been raised as a foster child by a relative of Lizzie Casaway - Mack Hamilton of Perry Hill, Texas. The Hamiltons were a troubled family - many of them died violent deaths - and McWilliams lost track of them after moving to San Antonio. In the spring of 1911, he received a letter and then a visit from a woman named Ballard, a distant family member. She told McWilliams that Lizzie lived less than a quarter mile from him and that she was married to a black man.

McWilliams didn't believe it at first and went to go and see Lizzie for himself. When he got to her house, he greeted her from the gate, and they talked for a few minutes. He could see her children through a window, playing in the house. According to what he told detectives, he remained angry about the fact that she'd married a black man until Lizzie told him about the abuse and abandonment that she'd suffered in her first marriage. Casaway had been kind to her, McWilliams said, and they had a happy life together.

Other witnesses didn't tell the same story that McWilliams did about his meeting with Lizzie, however. Sheriff's detectives had been told of a visit that Lizzie had received the day before the murders. She recounted to a friend that "she had been urged to leave her husband and children but refused to do so." This witness had offered the information anonymously, refusing to give her name, even for the reward. They also received other information from a neighbor named James Nelson that McWilliams "talked about having put five negroes out of the way, that three of them were buried in the same hole."

After McWilliams was arrested his home was searched and a letter was found that matched the paper and handwriting of an anonymous letter that had been mailed to the sheriff's department. That letter - addressed to Sheriff Tobin and Richard Campbell - had been dismissed as the work of a "crank." The letter writer claimed responsibility for the murders and wrote of his hatred for Sheriff Tobin. It was, Tobin believed, the work of a disturbed mind. The letter was printed in the newspaper two days after McWilliams's arrest:

To the Sheriff of Bexar County, and also to R.A. Campbell, lawyer - I understand that you all are in search for the man that killed the Louis Casaway family. Well, I am the man, and I am going to give you trouble in catching me, and whenever you run across me there will be trouble on your hands. I am no negro. I am a full-blooded white man, and again, I never wrote this. I had it done by a man that is today about three hundred miles from here, and I am in the city of

San Antonio now. So catch me if you can and there will be
trouble on your hands, because I am in a dangerous place and
I mean to kill the first one that tackles me about the matter,
so you can all pop your whip and get busy. I am ready to die
at any time, so look out.

I had a right to kill that family, and if you ever catch
me I will explain it to you.

McWilliams was held in the country jail and when he appeared for a hearing the next week most of the people in the courtroom were neighbors of the Casaways. McWilliams laughed out loud several times during the testimony and his "aged wife, sitting at his side, also seemed to find considerable merriment in the proceedings."

When he returned to court the following day he was escorted by sheriff's deputies through a massive crowd of spectators outside the courthouse. By the time he reached the courtroom his demeanor was drastically changed from the day before. His face was pale, and his hands shook. There was no laughter from him on the second day, but he did suffer from a severe coughing spell when the still-bloody ax that had killed the Casaways was brought into the courtroom.

A federal marshal testified that McWilliams, whom he considered a nuisance after several visits to his office, had bragged to him several times that he knew who had killed the Casaways. But when he reminded McWilliams that he could receive a $500 reward from the sheriff's office for that information, the other man replied, "I wouldn't tell Tobin anything. I have as much use for him as I do a bedbug, and you know what to do with a bedbug - kill it!"

After two days of hearings, Judge Dwyer granted McWilliams bail on murder charges -- $1,000 per victim.

Unable to raise $5,000, he returned to jail until a new grand jury could be empaneled later in the year.

But William McWilliams never stood trial for the slayings. The reason for this remains unclear, but charges against him were likely dismissed when ax murders continued across Texas and Louisiana while McWilliams was safely locked up in jail.

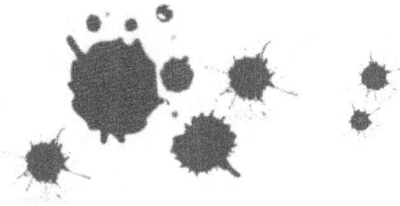

While McWilliams was facing charges, the authorities in Texas had been contacted by Louis LaCoste, the Sheriff of Lafayette Parish in Louisiana. He had some information that he wanted to share with Sheriff Tobin and the other investigators about a string of similar murders back home.

When LaCoste heard about the slaughter in San Antonio, he came to believe that the same killer had been involved in earlier murders in Louisiana.

And he was right.

2. "WOMAN AND CHILDREN KILLED"

RAYNE, LOUISIANA – NOVEMBER 13, 1909

Of all the murders that I believe can be linked to the Axman, the least is known about the Opelousas murders that occurred in 1909. Sheriff LaCoste believed that they could be linked to the murders that happened later - and I believe he was right - but there remains no explanation as to why the killer did not strike again for more than a year. There's a good chance that the murders in Rayne, Louisiana were his first, so perhaps he had to work up the nerve to kill again. Or perhaps he was sick, or more likely, in jail for a time. Whatever the reason for the delay, he did kill again, and the next time he slaughtered two families in less than one month.

Located in Acadia Parish, the small town of Rayne was a quiet Southern Pacific railroad town in 1909. It had been started shortly after the Civil War when a French immigrant named Jules Pouppe started a small mercantile store along the Old Spanish Trail, which traveled from New Orleans into Texas. A small community grew around the station that was dubbed "Pouppeville" in honor of the first resident.

Around 1880, word reached the settlement that a railroad line was being built to connect New Orleans with the West Coast. A railroad doctor named William Cunningham purchased lots along the proposed route of the railroad line, about a mile north of Pouppeville. Merchants followed and the entire community moved along with them, establishing Rayne - named for a railroad engineer - in 1883.

Rayne, Louisiana in the early 1900s

The town grew slowly in the years that followed. Banks, newspapers, hotels, stores, and restaurants opened in the community, but it was one eatery - the Rayne Drop Inn - that put the small town on the national map. The owner, Donat Pucheau, was a French immigrant and had come to Rayne because of its proximity to undeveloped lands for hunting. He created a menu of wild game and frog legs, which soon became a delicacy. He began shipping "iced down" frog legs to New Orleans, exchanging them for fine wines and cheeses, and soon people were flocking to Rayne to indulge in the rare dish at Pucheau's table.

Other restaurateurs followed Pucheau's example and Rayne became gripped in what local historians refer to as "frog mania" in the early 1900s. Travelers on the railroad stopped in Rayne for brief layovers so that they could walk the town, eat in the restaurants, and marvel at the "frog pen" in the town square where as many as 15,000 frogs were kept at one time. Rayne is still referred to today as the "frog capital of the world."

It was during this boom time of tourism in the town that the murders of Edna Opelousas occurred in what was known as the "negro quarter of town."

In the early morning hours of November 13, 1909, neighbors near her home were awakened by the screams of Edna's three small children. Edna lived in a small shack - no more than 10x12 feet - in the front yard of her father's home. There were neighbors on both sides of the lot, within 20 feet of the shack, and a "negro church" was less than 50 feet away. There were no witnesses to the attack - but dozens of people saw the result of it.

The screams began just after 1:00 a.m. Neighbors who were startled from their beds rushed to the house and hurried inside. There was, as the *Daily Signal* newspaper noted, "blood and brains scattered all over the little room."

Edna - referred to initially as a "negro woman" but later and more accurately as a mulatto - lived alone in the home with her three children, ranging in age from nine to four. Edna was found dead at the scene. Her head had been bashed open by the blunt side of an ax. The children had also been hit with the ax but were still alive when neighbors arrived. The blood-covered ax had been left behind at the scene as a bloody reminder of the crime.

Notice was sent to the police and a doctor was summoned to care for the children. He pronounced their cases as "hopeless," and all three of them died later that morning.

Sheriff Louis Fontenot and Coroner C. Hines Webb drove to Rayne to investigate the murder later that morning.

A coroner's inquest was held and before the day was out sheriff's deputies had already made arrests in the case.

Even though no one had seen the attacks occur there were possible witnesses to what happened before and after the crime. According to Edna's sister - whose name was never mentioned in any of the reports I could find - she had been asleep at her father's nearby home when she was awakened by the sound of Edna's door being opened. She looked out the window and said she saw a man going inside. She cried out to her sleeping father and, a few moments later, heard the children screaming in the shack.

Before her father could get to Edna's house the killer fled and was seen by a neighbor next door. He was running south - toward the railroad tracks, by the way - with his hat in his hand.

The yard was too poorly lit for either the neighbor or Edna's sister to describe or possibly identify the man they saw.

Sheriff Fontenot questioned everyone in the neighborhood and soon learned of neighbors who had grievances with Edna. By that afternoon he had taken George Washington, his wife, America, and their daughter, Estelle, to jail for questioning. He charged them with having knowledge of the crime. Estelle was an easy target. She had recently been arrested for assaulting Edna Opelousas, during which she had threatened to "use an ax" on her.

The family was questioned extensively, but it soon became obvious that there was nothing to connect them to the murders. The charges were dropped, and they were released.

Another arrest followed a few days later. On Thursday, November 18 Houston Goodwill was arrested in New Iberia by Deputy Sheriff Lyman Clark.

Goodwill was Edna's brother-in-law, married to her unnamed sister, and until recently he and his family had been staying in the shack where Edna was killed. Edna and her children had been staying in the neighboring house with her father. About a week before the murders Goodwill and his wife got into an argument and Edna's sister had kicked him out of the house. It was alleged that Goodwill was angry about being thrown out and he had threatened to kill his wife. The family was so worried that he might make good on his threats that Edna and her children moved into the shack, and her sister and her children moved into the house with their father.

If Goodwill were the killer, this would have been a fatal mistake.

Investigators surmised that Goodwill returned to the property on the night of the murders to get his revenge and did not discover who was sleeping in the bed that he'd once occupied with his wife until after he had struck the first blow, killing Edna. When the children were awakened and began to scream, he had killed them, too, hoping to avoid detection.

It was a good theory, and Goodwill certainly seemed the perfect candidate for a revenge killing, but he didn't do it. He was violent, mean, and a heavy drinker but, apparently, was not a killer. The police couldn't make the charges stick and Houston Goodwill was also released.

The Opelousas case soon grew cold and the police moved on to other things. It was mentioned a few times in newspaper stories that followed other similar murders, but, over time, it was largely forgotten.

The murders in Rayne remain unsolved.

3. "BRUTAL MURDER OF NEGRO FAMILY"

CROWLEY, LOUISIANA – JANUARY 25, 1911

More than a year after the murders in Rayne, the Axman returned to Acadia Parish - and into the jurisdiction of Sheriff Fontenot. Once again, the investigation would lead to nowhere. Only one suspect - whose name was never released - was ever seriously questioned, and he was released. These murders were just as baffling as the ones that had occurred in Rayne.

Although larger than Rayne, Crowley was still a small town in 1911. Known for its rice farms, it was also located along the railroad line and was named for Pat Crowley, an Irish railroad man. The town was founded in 1886 by C.C. Duson and W.W. Duson, the general manager of the Southwest Louisiana Land Company. His daughter, Maime, later married Percy Lee Lawrence, who founded the First National Bank of Crowley. The seven-story bank building was once the tallest building between Houston and New Orleans. It attracted scores of other businesses to the town, including mercantile stores, hotels, and restaurants.

With the rice farms and the service industries in town, there was a great need for employees, like farmworkers, cooks, porters, janitors, and liverymen - all jobs then held almost exclusively in the South by African American workers.

The jobs were essential but low-paying and most workers lived in low income, ramshackle housing in West Crowley, a part of the city that was known by both residents and in the newspapers as "Coontown."

The Byers murders of January 1911 would be the first of the Axman's murders to occur in Crowley's "Coontown" - they would not be the last.

The murders took place in the early morning hours of Wednesday, January 25. They were not discovered until Thursday afternoon when a young neighbor girl came to the home of Walter Byers, his wife, Sylvinia, and their six-year-old son. She found the door locked, and when she knocked there was no answer. That was when she noticed the terrible smell. Frightened, she returned home and told her mother, who then made a telephone call to the police. Officer Ballew at the station was told to come to 605 Western Avenue, "where it was believed a murder had been committed."

The first officers at the scene found the entire family in one bed in the small home. All were black and all had been murdered with an ax, probably while they were asleep. The newspaper clearly stated, "the murderer left no clue behind that the police have discovered."

The victims were lying in bed with their skulls split open. The bed was covered with blood and there were bloody footprints on the floor. The doors had all been locked from the inside, forcing Bellew and two other officers to break open the front door. It was later learned that the murderer had entered the house through a window.

All three of the Byers had been struck only one time with the ax - which was found propped up at the foot of the bed - but that had been enough. The little boy had been left at the feet of his parents, turned sideways across the bed.

A washbowl on the stand in the room was half-filled with bloody water, revealing that the killer had washed his hands before he left the scene. Bloody footprints were also found on the floor in front of the washstand. A basin shoved beneath it was half-filled with blood.

Coroner C. Hines Webb was called to the scene, and he met with local officers Chief of Police Burt, Marshal Lyons, and Officer Bellew. When they began interviewing the neighbors, they soon found that the Byers family had no known enemies. Walter Byers was an industrious man with a good reputation who worked for one of the rice mills in town. He was known as a quiet, peaceable man who served as the secretary of the Colored Baptist Church. He had been seen on Tuesday afternoon coming home from work, and Sylvinia was last seen about 6:30 that evening.

No one was seen entering or leaving their home on Tuesday night or early Wednesday morning. The coroner estimated that they had been dead about 36 hours when they were discovered.

But who had done it?

No one knew of any trouble between Walter and Sylvinia or between the couple and anyone else. The murders seemed to be completely random - which made them even more terrifying - but they weren't. It was impossible for the lawmen not to notice the similarity of the crime to the one that had occurred in nearby Rayne. Soon the connection between them would become much more obvious.

In late January 1911, though, the murders were a mystery. Only one arrest was ever made and all charges against the unknown man were eventually dropped.

The murders of the Byers family remain unsolved.

4. "CRUSHED WITH TERRIBLE BLOWS"

LAFAYETTE, LOUISIANA – FEBRUARY 25, 1911

Less than one month after the Byers murders the Axman struck again, just east of Crowley in the town of Lafayette. The previous murders had been horrific and tragic, but now things had become downright strange.

The killer was no longer confining himself to small towns. Lafayette was the fourth largest city in the state, but like all the others it was also a railroad town. It had been settled by French, Spanish, and Acadian colonists as early as the mid-eighteenth century. In the 1820s it became a proper settlement with the long name of St. Jean du Vermilionville. That was eventually shortened to Vermilionville.

In 1823, the Louisiana legislature formed a new parish named after the Marquis de Lafayette, the hero of the American Revolution, who was soon undertaking a grand tour of the United States at the bequest of President James Monroe. In 1869 a charter was introduced to rename the town of Vermilionville to Lafayette. There was a problem with this plan, though -- there was already a town in Louisiana, a suburb of New Orleans, called Lafayette. The plan was put on the backburner until 1884 when New Orleans incorporated the other Lafayette into its boundaries. This allowed Vermilionville to finally change its name. By then it was already the hub city of the region with a multitude of businesses, a growing population, and railroad station.

In the early morning hours of February 25, 1911, it became the scene of another of the Axman's murders when four people were slaughtered in the city's poor African American neighborhood.

Word of the murders reached Lafayette Parish Sheriff Louis LaCoste shortly after 7:00 a.m. that morning. LaCoste summoned several of his men and they went down to the small Vermilion Street home of the Andrus family - located just steps away from the railroad tracks. When LaCoste arrived, he found that the Deputy Coroner, Dr. L.O. Clark was already there. Clark took LaCoste on a gruesome tour of the home, which belonged to Alexander Andrus, his wife, Mimi, their three-year-old son, Joachim, and their 11-month-old daughter, Agnes.

The house - not much more than a shack - had only one bed. The entire family had been sleeping in it when they were killed.

There was blood everywhere. It soaked the bedsheets, spattered the walls, puddled on the floor, and had been sprayed across the ceiling - likely when the Axman had swung his weapon back to strike the next blow. According to the newspapers, "The head of each member of the family was crushed with terrible blows, their brains spattered all over the room, and their bodies horribly tortured."

But it was what the killer had then done with the bodies that convinced Sheriff LaCoste that he should reach out to the authorities in San Antonio about the Casaway murders at a time when police departments rarely cooperated between adjoining jurisdictions, let alone across state lines.

It was also what probably haunted LaCoste for the rest of his days.

The Andrus house, where five victims of the killer were slain in late February 1912. This was not the first time that "religious" elements had appeared at the crime scenes and would not be the last.

The Axman had made some "adjustments" to the bodies after he had killed them. On the floor next to the bed, he had placed the bodies of the two Andrus children. Then, he had arranged the bodies of Alexander and Mimi in a position of kneeling, so that it looked as though they were praying over the bodies of the toddler and infant. Mimi's hand had been placed so that it rested on her husband's shoulder. It was no wonder that LaCoste came to believe that there was a "religious fanatic" at work.

The Andrus family had no known enemies. Alexander was considered a "hard-working man" who was liked and respected in the city's black community. He had been employed at the Southern Pacific Railroad roundhouse in Lafayette for about two years.

There are conflicting reports of who discovered the body. One newspaper stated that they were found on the morning of February 25 by Mimi's mother. Another reported that the bodies were found by Mimi's brother, Lezime Felix.

In the end, it really doesn't matter who discovered the crime scene, but it's likely that whoever it was, never forgot what they saw that morning.

Sheriff LaCoste almost immediately ruled out robbery as the motive. The Andrus family was very poor, and nothing appeared to have been stolen or was missing from the house, according to witnesses. Interestingly, in this case, the ax the killer used was not found at the scene. He'd apparently taken it with him this time.

According to Deputy Coroner Clark, the murders had taken place early in the morning of February 25. It had been a cold February night and the bodies were still slightly warm. That was about as scientific as crime scene analysis got in Louisiana in 1911.

LaCoste deduced that an unknown person, or persons, had entered the house sometime after midnight, using an unlocked kitchen door. An ax had been used to strike the heads of the sleeping parents and little boy. After that, LaCoste believed the killer had murdered the little girl while she was in her nearby cradle. The killer, or killers, then arranged the bodies into their prayerful poses before exiting the house through the kitchen door in the rear.

LaCoste was determined to solve the case. He was disturbed by it and refused to stop looking for the killer or any clews --- as "clues" was spelled at the time - as to that person's identity. But the investigation quickly fizzled out. There were no forensic experts in those days. Fingerprint collection and comparison was just getting started and was limited to larger city police departments. There was also little cooperation between various law enforcement agencies in the state, but that would soon change.

Lafayette Parish Sheriff
Louis LaCoste

Suspects were questioned and then dismissed, and the case went rapidly nowhere. And then LaCoste caught a break when he learned that an "escaped lunatic" from Pineville was loose in the area. Who but a madman could have committed such an atrocious crime? On February 27 two deputies tracked down the asylum inmate, Garcon Godfry, at his mother's home in Maurice and arrested him. But Garcon - despite his mental condition and violent tendencies - had an airtight alibi for the time of the murder. He had still been locked up at the asylum. The deputies kept him at the local jail until he could be returned to the hospital.

Weeks passed and the search for the killer turned cold. Then, almost by accident, LaCoste learned of other crimes that bore an eerie resemblance to the Andrus murders. He first learned about the murders in Rayne and Crowley, and then a local man informed LaCoste about an article that he'd seen in a Texas newspaper about a San Antonio family that had been murdered in their sleep on March 21.

LaCoste managed to track down the report. The Texas article said that a "nearly white" negro family of five by the name of Casaway had been butchered in their home in San Antonio. They had all been struck in the head while sleeping. There was no bizarre posing of the bodies but - and I saved this to reveal to the readers after the Andrus murders - the Casaway family had been moved and arranged so that they were placed in order from largest to smallest. Louis was on one end of the bed, and the youngest child, Alfred, was on the opposite. The killer had then, the newspaper reported, covered them with blankets, as if to send them off to sleep.

As LaCoste read the article he realized that after killing families in Rayne and Crowley the murderer had struck in Lafayette and then crossed the state line to San Antonio. He believed the crimes were all connected, and he must have been mortified to reach this conclusion. The term "serial killer" would not come into use for several more decades, and even the idea of a "repeat murderer," as they were then dubbed, was a foreign concept. Such things only happened in the large cities - not in rural towns of Louisiana and Texas.

As a sheriff of the early 1900s, he was used to dealing with drunks, assaults, and even the occasional killing, but not with elaborate multiple murders with seemingly bizarre elements to them. He struggled with the motive behind the murders and even the logistics of them. LaCoste became sure they were connected - but how? And why did the killer commit murders in three towns in Louisiana and then travel 450 miles to San Antonio to commit another? Soon he would realize that the cities where the murders occurred were all connected by the railroads, which explained how the killer likely traveled, but the motive behind the murders remained a mystery.

LaCoste sent a telegram to the authorities in San Antonio seeking details about the crime scene in their city. He asked about the murders, and, in return, he shared details about the crime in Lafayette and the earlier murders in Rayne and Crowley. LaCoste was undoubtedly the first lawman to connect the four murders and to theorize that the Axman was traveling by train, but it would soon be shared by other lawmen who were working on the various cases. As the *Lafayette Advertiser* noted, "The crimes are so alike that they may be the work of the same terrible monster."

LaCoste certainly believed that they were, and he became almost obsessed with the murders. He believed that he only needed to find the common thread between all of them and the murders could be solved. That common thread, he knew, was a single killer - a man who had committed four sets of murders across two states. LaCoste was certain he would find that man in Louisiana.

And that's when he found Raymond Barnabet.

5. "NEGRO MURDERER"

THE ARREST AND TRIAL OF RAYMOND BARNABET

After months of false leads and dwindling evidence, LaCoste became focused on a man named Raymond Barnabet, an African American sharecropper and small-time criminal. He came to the attention of investigators after an argument with a woman he lived with who appears in records only as "Diana." The two had lived together in a sharecropper's cabin on a cotton farm between Crowley and Rayne, which they also shared with Raymond's children, son Zepherin and daughter, Clementine.

After a falling out, Diana went to live with a friend and started talking badly about Raymond. She even claimed that he had told her some terrible things about the recent ax murders. Whatever it was that he said, Diana told her friend that it convinced her that Raymond was the killer. The friend passed this information along to the police and led to Raymond's arrest. LaCoste and several deputies found him picking cotton in the fields and handcuffed him on the spot.

LaCoste began grilling Barnabet relentlessly about the Andrus murders, but Raymond insisted that he was not the murderer and that he knew nothing about the case. The sheriff then had Diana brought into the station. He asked her for details about the murders and demanded to know what she had told her friend about Raymond's possible involvement with them. She spoke a great deal about Raymond - mostly about his petty life of crime and his cruelty - but she refused to implicate him directly when LaCoste questioned her. She claimed that her friend had misunderstood what she had told her and said that Raymond had been drunk when he was talking about the murders and didn't know what he was saying. Apparently, whatever hard feelings she'd had toward Raymond had been smoothed over between the time of the argument and the man's arrest.

LaCoste realized that he was getting nowhere with Diana's interview, so he had Raymond's estranged wife and his two children brought in for questioning. All three of them were quick to blame Raymond for the murders. In fact, they had so much to say that the interviews lasted for two days. Raymond was, they said, "very definitely" the slayer of the Andrus family. They were so definite that LaCoste was somewhat troubled by their statements. When he asked them about their motive for turning on Raymond, they all said almost exactly the same thing - to spare other innocents from the atrocity that had been visited on the Andrus family. When he asked them for a motive, each of them told the sheriff that Raymond was involved in an ongoing feud with Alexander Andrus. The two men were enemies, they said, even though the sheriff had found no evidence of Andrus having any enemies during his investigation. But the Barnabet family insisted it was true. Raymond, enraged by an argument, must have killed the man and his family in their sleep one night. Together with his drunkenness and criminal history, it was obvious that he was the murderer.

Did LaCoste have doubts about their story? Possibly. He likely found the way they had handed him a perfect case almost too convenient. Their statements - especially the part about sparing other innocents - seemed rehearsed. And what about the other murders? The family claimed to only have knowledge of the one set of murders. They know nothing about the crimes in Rayne or Crowley, let alone in San Antonio, which LaCoste believed was the work of the same killer.

After the second day of questioning the Barnabet family, Sheriff LaCoste went to see the Lafayette Parish District Attorney, John J. Robira. There are no details about what exactly was said between the two men, although there must have been a lot of discussion about the case against Raymond Barnabet and the family's testimony against him. Did LaCoste express his doubts about the authenticity of the testimony? Perhaps he did. It is also possible that the district attorney was just as eager to wrap up the case as the sheriff was and tried to alleviate his concerns by interviewing the three witnesses himself.

The following day, Robira spoke to the Barnabets, and he told reporters that he found their credibility and their statements to be very convincing. All of them had agreed to testify against Raymond at trial, and Robira was especially encouraged by statements from Raymond's 19-year-old daughter, Clementine. He was anxious to get her in front of the jury.

Robira also added that all three of the Barnabets were "of good community standing" - a statement that he would soon regret.

After presenting the case to a grand jury, Robira charged Raymond Barnabet with four counts of first-degree murder. Excitement rippled through the community and, perhaps fearing a lynching, Sheriff LaCoste contacted Sheriff Fontenot in Acadia Parish to temporarily house Barnabet in his jail until he went on trial in Lafayette.

On the day that Raymond was transferred to the Acadia Parish jail, the *Crowley Signal* ran a story about the accused killer. In the article, it was claimed that Barnabet and Alexander Andrus had once worked together at the Southern Pacific coal chutes and speculated that a disagreement between the two men might have led to the murders. There was, of course, no hard evidence to back this up, nor were there any witnesses who claimed the two men had been enemies except for Barnabet's wife and children. But it was in the newspaper, locals agreed, so it must be the truth.

Raymond Barnabet's trial began in October 1911. He was represented by a court-appointed attorney named George P. Sessley and two associates, Jerome E. Poche and J.J. Fournet. They were facing District Attorney Robira for the state. The crowd - both black and white - was packed into the courtroom, eager to see what was going to happen to Barnabet, who appeared unkempt and disinterested in the trial.

The jury was made up of 12 white men.

The district attorney had three star witnesses for the trial - Dr. L.O. Clark, the parish's deputy coroner, and Zepherin and Clementine Barnabet. Dr. Clark provided the jury with gruesome accounts of the blood-soaked crime scene. His testimony brought gasps of shock from spectators in the courtroom. Several women burst into tears at his description of little Agnes, murdered in her crib. The men in the jury box squirmed uncomfortably, faces pale at the graphic picture painted by the coroner. Eyes fell on Raymond, slumped at the defense table, and they narrowed in anger.

Clementine followed Dr. Clark to the stand. Newspapers would later state that it was her testimony that truly convicted her father. It would all be backed up by her brother, Zepherin. In news accounts, it was said, "Their testimony made men shudder." One after another they testified that their father came home between 2:00 a.m. and 4:00 a.m. when the Andrus murdered occurred. In a rage, he woke up his children and forced them out of bed. He had blood all over his clothes, his face, and in his hair. Raymond forced Clementine to wash his bloody clothing and warned his family to keep quiet about it - or else. Zepherin confirmed his sister's story, even adding that their father had bragged that he "killed the whole damn Andrus family." They both told the jury that they feared for their lives if their father did not go to prison.

It should come as no surprise that the jury returned four guilty verdicts against Raymond Barnabet on October 21, 1911. Judge William Campbell then called for a short recess before sentencing. As soon as the courtroom filled again, George Sessley, Raymond's public defender, requested that his client be granted a new trial. Raymond had not been able to testify on his own behalf because he was drunk. He had not realized until now, Sessley told the judge, that his client had come to court each day under the influence of alcohol.

Judge Campbell was furious, shouting at the bailiff, the jailer, and the sheriff for not realizing that the prisoner had been drinking. He announced that he would take the defense's motion into consideration and adjourned until the following morning. At that time, the judge stated that Barnabet would be granted a new trial during the next term of court, which would be months away.

But while Raymond Barnabet was behind bars waiting for his new trial, another brutal ax murder occurred.

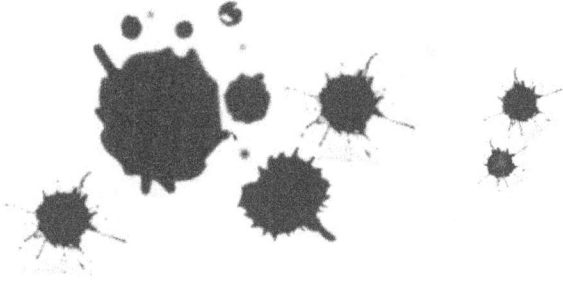

8. "BUTCHERY OF HUMAN BEINGS"

LAFAYETTE, LOUISIANA – NOVEMBER 27, 1911

The home of the Randall family was located on Lafayette Street, near the cotton mill, in the town's "black district." Unlike the home of the Andrus family, it was not a shack. Norbert Randall worked as a butler for a local white family and was able to afford a three-room house on his salary. He took good care of his wife, Azema, and their five children - Albert, age 8; Rene, age 6; Norbert, Jr., age 5; Agnes, who was 2, and an older girl who was never named in reports who was age 10.

The murders were discovered on the morning of November 27 when the oldest daughter returned home from spending the night at her uncle's house. She found the kitchen door open and when she entered, she discovered her parents and her siblings in two blood-soaked beds. All of them were dead. They had been bludgeoned to death with the blunt side of an ax - except for Norbert, who had been shot in the head. Norbert, Azema, and Agnes were found in one of the beds. The three boys were found piled at the end of the other. The ax - which had been washed off - was leaning against the footboard of the parents' bed. When investigators arrived, they puzzled over rags that had been stuffed into the keyholes of the front and back doors.

The young girl immediately ran next door to a neighbor's house, wailing in fear, and a call was placed to the police station. Sheriff LaCoste and several deputies rushed to

The Randall House on Lafayette Street, where six people were
murdered just days after Raymond Barnabet's trial

the scene, hoping to find some evidence, but the rain had been
falling for hours, wiping out any footprints that might have
been left outside.

Inside the house, nothing appeared to be disturbed.
Again, robbery didn't seem to be the motive. Eerily, it turned
out that Norbert Randall and Alexander Andrus were
brothers-in-law. The crime appeared similar to the murders at
the Andrus home - aside from Norbert being shot in the head
- but something about it was bothering Sheriff LaCoste.

There is no clear record of how he came to a decision,
but by noon on November 27, he had arrested Clementine
Barnabet for the Randall murders. She was now living only a
block away from the Randall home, and the *Lafayette
Advertiser* said only that "certain things led the sheriff to
arrest her." He and his men arrested not only Clementine but
her brother, Zepherin, and two other African Americans who
were at the house when the lawmen arrived.

Likely, Sheriff LaCoste's concerns about the stories told by the Barnabets at their father's trial had continued to eat at him. During Raymond's trial, the defense brought up the questionable reputations of Zepherin and Clementine. Their neighbors had even described them as "filthy, shifty, and degenerate." And there was one other thing that had been bothering the sheriff since he had arrested Raymond at his home - officers had discovered blood on Clementine's clothes. During her father's trial, she claimed that Raymond had wiped the blood from the murder scene on them, but Sheriff LaCoste doubted her version of the story. His doubts are likely what caused him to so quickly arrest her on the day of the Randall murders.

When deputies arrested Clementine, they searched the house where she was staying and found clothing that had been given to her by her employer, a white woman named Mrs. Jane Guidry. She would later identify the garments as having once belonged to her. According to a newspaper report, the clothing was "a complete suit of woman's clothes, saturated with blood and covered with human brains." They also found that the front door latch was covered with dried blood.

It was later discovered that Zepherin had an alibi for the night of the Randall murders, but Clementine did not. She refused to confess to the crime and maintained that the blood on the clothing was menstrual blood. Sheriff LaCoste sent the clothing to Louisiana State Chemist Abraham L. Metz in New Orleans for testing. The test took nearly two months but confirmed what Sheriff LaCoste believed - the blood was not menstrual blood. It was human, and it was mixed with particles of brain and fragments of skull.

Clementine Barnabet was a killer.

"I have sufficient evidence to convict her," LaCoste told reporters, "but I am not satisfied that the fiendish acts were not committed by one person alone, and I am now on the trail of her alleged accomplices."

And I think he was right. I believe that Clementine - along with someone else - committed the Randall murders. And I believe that her accomplices committed more murders after that - murders that have been confused with those committed by the Axman. The next murders occurred in January 1912 and were meant to make it look as though Clementine was innocent of the Randall killings. She couldn't have committed them; it was supposed to appear because she was locked up in jail.

When that didn't work, she gave the police one of the strangest confessions ever recorded in the annals of American crime, as we'll soon see.

Meanwhile, the Axman was still out there. And while he hadn't committed the Randall murders or the one that followed - he would certainly kill again.

7. "GHASTLY CRIME DISCOVERED"

CROWLEY, LOUISIANA – JANUARY 18, 1912

Murder struck again in the "Coontown" section of Crowley on January 18, but this time the Axman wasn't the one who swung the weapon. He hadn't killed the Randalls, and he didn't kill the Warners either.

These killers were someone else altogether.

Marie Warner, a 30-year-old woman of mixed race, lived with her children in a part of the neighborhood between Sixth and Seventh Streets called the "Promised Land." The name was meant to be sarcastic. The residents were poverty-stricken, barely getting by with the menial jobs that could find. Marie and her children lived in a four-room shack that had been divided into two apartments. One entrance faced the street and the other opened into the back yard. The Warners lived in the rear section of the shack - and the killers gained entrance to her two rooms through the back door, which was draped in shadows during the early morning hours.

Marie had three children - Pearl, age 9; Garey, age 7; and Harriet, age 5. All the children were at home with her on the night of January 17. Marie had been separated from her husband for almost four years. The police later learned that he was living and working in Texas.

Just before noon on January 18, Marie's mother, Harriet Crane, came over to the Warner house to visit with her daughter and grandchildren. She went to the back door of the two-flat shack and knocked, but there was no answer. It

Marie Warner's home in 1912

is unknown why she did not open the door and go inside. It was soon discovered to be unlocked.

Instead, Harriet crossed the street to the home of a family friend, Dorsey Berdsong, and asked him if he had seen Marie or the children. He said that he hadn't and told her that he thought that was strange. He usually saw them up and about early in the morning. The two of them went back across the street together and knocked again at the back door. That was when they realized that the door was not only unlocked but standing partially open.

Harriet pushed the door and it yawned open, revealing nothing but darkness and shadows inside. It was eerily quiet and there was a thick, coppery smell coming from inside.

They were both too afraid to enter.

Just then, a friend of Dorsey's named Ben Robinson passed by on the street. Dorsey flagged him down and explained what was happening. Harriet pleaded with him to go into the house and check on her family. Ben stepped cautiously into the apartment, trying to see in the gloomy

A newspaper photograph showing the interior of the Warner house after the murders were discovered.

light. There was a bed pushed into one corner of the room and he could see something there, under blankets that looked as though they had been smeared with paint. As he took two more steps, he realized what he was looking at - the mangled remains of the four occupants of the flat, twisted on the bed that was covered in blood. As the *Daily Signal* would later report, the bodies were "across the bed" but face down in a curious manner.

Ben Robinson ran for his life.

The police were summoned to the scene and soon investigators were searching diligently for clews inside and outside of the house. Among them was Sheriff Louis Fontenot. This was the third ax murder scene that he was forced to investigate. We must wonder if he noticed anything different about this one - because I believe it was not the work of the same killer.

From the appearance of the house, it seemed that at least some of the victims were killed in the back room and their bodies moved to the front room to be placed together, face down on the bed. There were no signs of struggle, so investigators assumed they had been killed in their sleep. Each of them had been struck by the blunt side of a common ax. The ax itself was found propped against the wall in the room where the bodies were discovered.

Deputy Coroner Dr. M.L. Hoffpauir held an inquest at the home on the afternoon of the murders but had no new information to offer the police. They concluded that the murders had taken place during the early morning hours, while the family was asleep. Tracks in the backyard suggested that more than one person was implicated in the crime - which was different than the other Crowley murder that had taken place one year before - but there was no way to be sure.

The house was put under guard while officers waited for bloodhounds to be brought in to try and follow the killer's trail. This was a common practice during a police investigation in that era. In fact, I'm surprised to have not seen mention of it after the earlier murders. Using dogs to try and follow a criminal's trail was one of the most advanced investigative techniques used in the late nineteenth and early twentieth centuries. Bloodhounds could be surprisingly accurate in tracking people over long distances and could often lead to further clews that would aid the investigation. In this case, though, recent rains had made the trail too muddled for the dogs to follow, and the search led nowhere.

This was the second set of murders in Crowley's "Coontown" in a year, and residents were shocked and frightened. Of course, no one realized that these murders were not the work of the same killer. But did it matter? Not to the neighbors of Marie Warner and everyone else who lived in the neighborhood. They were terrified - and their fears were about to get worse.

A few days later another massacre occurred. This time it was in Lake Charles, Louisiana, and the strange elements of this crime began the panic that would soon come to grip the African American community of the region.

The Axman, I believe, was back.

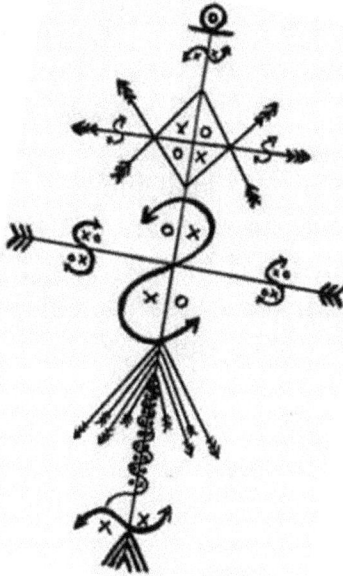

8. "FIVE ARE KILLED IN BEDS WITH AX"

LAKE CHARLES, LOUISIANA – JANUARY 22, 1912

Four days after the murders of Marie Warner and her three children, the slaughter of five people took place 53 miles west of Crowley in the community of Lake Charles. It wasn't a great distance for the killers of the Warner family to have traveled in four days -- or it would not have been if it was the same killers. I don't believe that it was. I'm convinced that the Warner murders were false "Axman" murders, meant to try and clear the name of Clementine Barnabet, who the police had arrested for the Randall murders back in November. If she was in jail and the murders continued, then she must be innocent of the other crime, too.

It didn't work because Clementine was not innocent. She was a killer and, quite possibly, a lunatic, although evidence of that was still to come.

I believe that the murders in Lake Charles were the work of the Axman, back on the rails, claiming new victims. He had been dormant - at least as far as we know, in Louisiana and Texas - since March of 1911, when he killed the Casaway family in San Antonio. It had been less than a year since he had killed, which was not unusual. There had been more time between the murders in Rayne in 1909 and the murder in Crowley in January 1911.

Where had he been during those months? There is no way to know. I surmised previously that he might have been injured or in jail, but it's also possible that he had been away from the area. I think it's feasible that the Axman worked for the railroad and traveled across the South and possibly as far as the West Coast. The murders he committed likely coincided with when he was in the South for work. The railroads offered him a way to flee in the wake of the murders and remain outside of the area while the police searched for clews.

Why did he only choose Louisiana and Texas for his killings? Perhaps he didn't. Could there have been other murders that might be linked to this same killer? Yes, quite possibly, even out west, but so far, additional murders have remained elusive.

Some researchers - the few that there are with these particular cases - believe that the murders in Lake Charles may have also been linked to the Randall and Warner murders and the attempts by Clementine's compatriots to clear her name. It's possible, but I don't believe that to be the case. If you remember back to the Andrus murders in February 1911, you might recall the first bizarre religious aspects that began to seep into the murders. The bodies of the parents had been placed in a kneeling position above the bodies of their dead children. Investigators had pondered whether a "religious zealot" was committing the murders.

At the crime scene in Lake Charles, there was religious symbolism left behind - as you'll soon see -- implying that a band of fanatics was responsible for the deaths. I think this was more of the Axman's work. Of all the murders that occurred between 1909 and 1912, the Lake Charles murder scene gets the most attention, simply because it was so strange. I think this was done on purpose. I think the Axman was showing his dominance over the black families of the region - and local law enforcement.

Why? Because someone had stolen attention away from him. I'm theorizing that the Axman was working somewhere out west when the reports of the Randall murders appeared in the newspapers. There was a conjecture that the murders were part of the same spree of killings that he had been responsible for. Then, the Warner murders occurred, which seemed to be part of the same string of murders.

The Axman couldn't stand the idea that someone else was taking credit for his murders and so he immediately struck, just four days later, and 53 miles away from the most recent massacre. And he went out of his way to leave all his signatures behind. He entered through a window. He killed everyone with the blunt side of an ax. No one was shot like Norbert Randall had been.

And then he left a message behind, just as he had done at the Andrus house.

He wanted to make sure that he got the credit for the crimes he committed, but unfortunately, it didn't work out as he'd planned. Clementine Barnabet would steal elements of his crime and mix them into the weird confession that she made in April 1912. Also, the police and the media would use some of the ingredients of the Lake Charles murders to create their own mixture of race, murder, mystery, Voodoo, and cults.

Thwarted again. Is it any wonder that the Axman just kept killing?

Felix Broussard and his family lived at 331 Rock Street on the north side of Lake Charles, which was, of course, the "black section" of town. The house was within 50 feet of the Kansas City Southern Railroad line and a short distance from the Lake Charles rice mill, where Felix worked. He also had a job at the Majestic Hotel in Lake Charles. He was described as a "good type of Negro" and an "industrious and intelligent man who lived happily with his wife and three children." He was about 50 years of age and lived in a three-room house with his wife, Matilda, and his three daughters, Louise, age 6, and twins, Elberta and Margaret, both age 3. The Broussards also had two grown daughters who no longer lived at home.

Felix was not as poor as most of the victims of the Axman. He and his wife owned several pieces of furniture, along with their small home. He was a responsible man who was concerned with the well-being of his family, as evidenced by the life insurance policies that he had. The family had only recently moved to Lake Charles but had become well acquainted with their neighbors.

Oddly, though, one newspaper report mentioned that Felix had said something strange to one of those neighbors on the day before the tragedy. Although no one in his family was ill, Felix had remarked to a friend that "they were all going home to glory and mighty soon." This remark - which may or may not have actually been said - led some to believe that Felix had a premonition about the impending slaughter of his family.

At some point during the early morning hours of January 22, the Axman entered the Broussard house through the kitchen window.

Felix and Matilda were asleep in the southwest room. All three of the children shared a bed in the adjoining northwest room. It was bitterly cold that night, especially for the Deep South, but Matilda had left a fire burning in the stove to keep the house warm. We have to wonder if the Axman warmed his hands in front of that stove before he went about his grisly work.

There's no way to know exactly what time the murders occurred, but their next-door neighbor, Victoria Northern, was up late cooking and took notice of the Broussard house the following morning. The back door of the Broussard house was standing open, letting in the chilly morning air. She told the newspaper:

I was up cooking until 1:30 o'clock last night. I saw the deceased family light a lamp about dark. Did not see them anymore after that.

When I got up this morning, I noticed the back door open and did not see anyone moving around in the house. I thought that a little strange and asked my husband to go over and knock on their door and call them.

He did, but no one answered. He said he would go in the house. I told him, 'No'; to get an officer.

Northern said that another neighbor, J.C. Thibodeaux, then came over to the house to see what was happening. While Victoria's husband had been checking on the Broussards, Thibodeaux's wife had come to the Northern house to borrow some milk. Mrs. Northern told her of her "uneasiness for the Broussard family."

It was Thibodeaux who first entered the Broussard house just after 10:00 a.m. He later said that he looked through the back door and saw "the leg of a child protruding" from under some blankets in the second bedroom. The children had been murdered while they slept, as had Felix and Matilda. Blood that didn't soak into their sheets pooled on the floor and ran into the kitchen area of the house.

Investigators were soon on the scene and found signs that showed that the Axman had entered through the kitchen window. When he left the house, he left through the back door, leaving it open behind him. Nothing appeared to have been stolen from the house, and only a few macabre clews were left behind.

In the southwest room, the police discovered the battered bodies of Felix and Matilda in their bed. The only sign of a struggle was that one of Matilda's arms was extended or thrown upward as if she might have been trying to protect herself from a blow. The murder weapon, the Broussards' own ax, was found under their bed. Blood and pieces of dark-colored hair were crusted onto the blunt side of the tool.

In the children's bedroom, the police found Louise, Elberta, and Margaret lying on the bed with their skulls crushed. One newspaper stated that they lay perfectly still, as they had when asleep. Another claimed that it looked as though the children "had struggled and had been thrown on the bed."

Adding to the horror of either scene, the Axman, after he had killed the three little girls, had placed a bucket below the bed where he could catch the blood that dripped from their wounds. Sheriff Davie Reid, the five-time elected sheriff of the parish, was concerned that the blood may have been collected for some sort of "ceremonial purpose." He feared the murders had been committed by a "religious maniac."

It's easy to understand why he believed this after he saw what was written on the inside of the family's back door. Some newspapers claimed the writing was in blood, while others stated it was in pencil. Either way, it was a chilling biblical message from Psalms 9:12 that read:

"When he maketh the inquisition for blood, he forgetteth not the cry of the humble."

The *Lake Charles Daily American-Press* wrote, "An inscription upon the door, thought to have been written there by the murderers, is significant of something sinister and fanatic in the mind of one who took the lives of the five innocent, colored people."

Over to the side of the inscription the killer had left further writing - "Human 5." No one knew what it meant. Was it the killer's name, or what he called himself? Was he designating that he'd killed five people? Were there five killers at work? The latter was the idea seized upon by the authorities, who recalled that investigators had found multiple tracks outside of the Warner house just days before. Of course, they didn't know that the recent murders in Crowley and the murders in Lake Charles were likely committed by different killers.

The meaning of the biblical verse to the killer - as well as the "Human 5" inscription - remain mysterious today.

Later, in a lurid and wildly speculative article in the *El Paso Herald*, a writer claimed that the hands of the victims were splayed apart to form an open hand after they were killed. He suggested that perhaps the open hands with five fingers offered the meaning behind the "Human 5." The problem is that this small detail from the crime scene was conjured up from his imagination. There is nothing in the record to suggest that anything had been done with the hands of the Broussards.

Meanwhile, two arrests were made in Crowley in connection with the Warner murders. They occurred soon after locals there learned of the murders in Lake Charles. One of those arrested was Joseph Wilkins, a Baptist preacher, and the other was Eliza Richards. Both were African American. The *Crowley Signal* noted, "The nature of the evidence against Wilkins and the woman has not been given out but is said to be strong."

Wilkins had been, as the newspaper said, "the pastor of St. Joseph's Baptist Church in Coontown for four of five years" after moving to Crowley from Arnaudville. Eliza Richards had also moved to town from Arnaudville around the same time. She was 25 years old and had been a close friend of Marie Warner.

The arrest of Wilkins and Richards came at a time when Crowley was nearly paralyzed with fear. Sheriff's deputies who had arrested the pair soon found themselves trying to protect them from an angry mob of black citizens who wanted justice for Marie Warner and her children. The situation was so volatile that Wilkins and Richards were secretly taken to holding cells in Lake Charles until they were placed on trial.

Their trials never happened, though. Whatever evidence the sheriff thought he had against the two was never disclosed. They were soon released and cleared of any connection to the crime. But their release - on top of two more murders within days of each other - had sent a ripple of fear through the black community.

According to headlines in the *Signal,* the inhabitants of the black neighborhoods were in a "state of terror" and dared not close their eyes at night. A reporter wrote:

This has thrown the colored population of Crowley into almost a panic, and unless something is done to stop the murders it is predicted that Coontown will soon be depopulated. In ever negro house in Crowley, lights are kept burning all night and the adult members of the family remain awake during the night, fearing to run the risk of a visit by the assassin who murders his victims by wholesale with an ax, sparing neither men, women not children...

Negro servants in Crowley are in a panic and few of them dare to be found on the streets after dark. The more superstitious believe that some supernatural agency is at work...

Things were bad, but they were soon going to get worse and not only in Crowley but throughout the entire region.

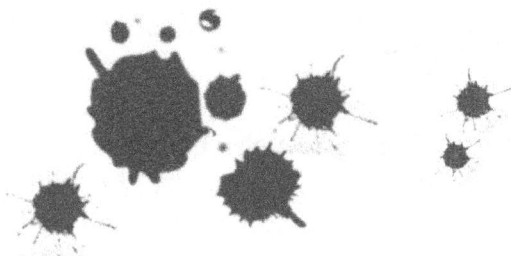

9. 'THE CHURCH OF THE SACRIFICE"

Just after the Broussard murders, the police made their next arrest - another African American preacher, Reverend King Harris, from Jennings, Louisiana. He was a suspect in the Randall murders, which had occurred in Lafayette in November, and was believed to be somehow connected to Clementine Barnabet through a cult that he led called the "Church of the Sacrifice." The police believed that this "Sacrifice Sect," as they called it, was "something on the order of the 'Council of God' sect in New Orleans."

The Council of God was an extremist black cult that was started by a disgraced minister named Albert Leon Antoine in the early 1900s. Antoine formed his church by using a group of older black men that he could send out into the community to attract poor, uneducated followers. The "prophets" as he called them, visited homes where residents were sick. They performed ceremonies at bedsides and then told the families that if the sick person was holy, they'd live. If they weren't, they'd die - so, they were right either way. Convinced of the healing powers of the prophets, Antoine gained new members for his church.

At the core of the church was a hatred for white people, which was, of course, why it was feared by white society. The church believed in heaven and hell but believed they were both here on earth. Heaven was inhabited by white people, who had wealth, security, and easy lives. Blacks were the inhabitants of hell, and they were punished with poverty, misery, and hard work. Antoine taught that through money and influence, blacks could overthrow the whites and enter heaven. This could only be accomplished through the annihilation of the white race. Once all the white people were dead, the poor and uneducated black people would take their place in heaven, and the educated, respected black population would become their slaves.

The Council of God did not recognize any "one" God but believed there was a spirit in every man. Antoine told his people that praying to God was foolish. "The nigger has been praying to God for 1,000 years and look what that's gotten him," he said.

The cult practiced polygamy and encouraged adultery. Marriages within the cult were celebrated with a ritual called the "Feast of the Coming Queen." It lasted for six days and ended with an orgy that included all the adult members of the sect.

The cult ended in 1907 after the arrest of many of its members. One night a marriage ceremony was being celebrated at the home of Edward Honore, one of the sect's leaders, and the noisy party disturbed some of the neighbors. A few local boys decided to throw bricks at the house. Since the cult had it written into their rules that anyone who disturbed a ceremony had to die, Honore and a few other officials went looking for the boys so they could kill them.

Unfortunately, the cultists found a man named John Sherman who was walking home alone. He'd had nothing to do with the rock-throwing incident. He proclaimed his innocence, but they didn't believe him. Sherman was able to get away from the men with just a few cuts from their knives, but the policeman that he reported the incident to was not so lucky.

The officer confronted the men and Honore slashed his throat. The 22-year-old policeman bled out in the street. The cultists fled but were soon tracked back to Honore's house. A shootout between the cult and the police lasted for nearly an hour. It ended when the cultists finally surrendered. As they were taken to jail an angry lynch mob had to be held back by the police.

Following arrests, indictments, and jail terms, the Council of God was destroyed, but it's easy to understand why its specter was still fresh in the minds of white police officers and newspaper reporters just five years later.

Even so, how did these small-town police officers come up with the idea of some strange cult that was mixed up in the murders that had been occurring across Louisiana for the past few years?

They had some help - from Clementine Barnabet.

Whether prompted by mental instability or the threat of "a night in jail and the third degree" from police officers in New Orleans, Clementine had started to hint at her role in not only the Randall murders but also to the murders of the Andrus family which her father had been (wrongly) convicted for. And it was all a conspiracy, she said, linked to the "Church of the Sacrifice." Members of the cult engaged in blood sacrifices under the protection of spells provided by Voodoo doctors.

She didn't explain how she'd been caught if she was "protected" by magic spells, but the white police officers readily seized on the idea of a black cult committing murders.

King Harris was arrested because they believed he was the leader - or at least a powerful member - of the sect. But Harris denied having anything to do with a "Sacrifice Cult." He was a Pentecostal preacher for a small congregation called the Christ Sanctified Church. He had never heard of the "Church of the Sacrifice," he said and was visibly upset to think that any of his sermons could have inspired a series of ax murders.

The only connection between Reverend Harris and the murders seemed to be that he had preached in Lafayette on the night of the Randall murders. There was also a rumor going around that the Randall family had been at the meeting, but there is no way to know if this was true. It's possible that this - along with the fact that someone had confused "Church of the Sacrifice" with the "Christ Sanctified Church" - was the only reason that Harris was brought in for questioning.

The arrest was widely circulated in the newspapers, and a short time later police officers in Lake Charles also made two arrests, thanks to tips from the authorities in Lafayette. The two men were Ed Jiles, who was described in the *Lake Charles Daily American-Press* as a "big crazy-acting negro," and Dr. A.E. Anderson. Both men were suspected of being tied to the mysterious "Church of the Sacrifice," and the authorities were determined to prove it.

Newspapers described Jiles as a "giant" after his arrest following the Broussard murders. When questioned he offered little information, if any, to the police about the Church of the Sacrifice. Jiles ended up in the "sweat box" - the era's version of an interrogation room - with the Lake Charles coroner, Dr. W.L. Fisher. Fisher stated that after the interview he believed that Jiles was insane. He said that the man had been making "inexplicable signs" with his hands when he asked him about his affiliation with the cult. Fisher also noted that Jiles could speak normally on general topics, but when he started asking him about "religion or lodges," Jiles became silent and refused to talk for the rest of the interview.

Fisher said to him, "Lots of people belong to churches or orders. There should be no reason why one should be averse to mentioning the name of the order or the church that one was connected with."

Jiles wouldn't say anything else, but Fisher said he continued to make strange hand signs and signals. When he asked him again about the church, the newspaper said, Jiles only nodded. Fisher didn't know if this was an affirmative answer or just another weird signal that Jiles was making.

The police were unable to link him to any crime, but they decided to keep him locked up because he was considered "too dangerous to be loose."

The other man arrested after the Broussard murders was Dr. A.E. Anderson, who wasn't really a doctor at all. He was a minister who had adopted the title to add some prestige to his followers. Anderson was arrested because of his "suspicious" travels to and from Lake Charles and Lafayette. The authorities had been told that he was a "verified" member of the Sacrifice cult, although no one ever revealed who had "verified" his membership.

What we do know is that Anderson was traveling around from one Southern Louisiana town to the next, "preaching a strange doctrine." He had only been back in Lake Charles for one day before the authorities arrested him.

Neither of the men was ever prosecuted for playing a part in the murders, but Reverend Harris's name would later intersect with the story of another suspect, linking him forever to the ghastly murders.

The murders were now numbering in the dozens, and despite the arrest of one suspect who was confessing to murder, and even more suspects behind bars, panic was starting to spread through the black communities of the region. It was reported in the *Lucy Meschacebe* newspaper that "many Lake Charles negroes have remained awake since the night of the murder, while not a few have organized into bands to watch while others sleep." To make matters worse, the *Lafayette Advertiser* said there had been more attempts to "enter negro homes." There were many "sensational tales circulated in regard to these attempts, which are greatly adding to the fright of the negroes." The *Pensacola Journal* related a story about a clueless white census taker in Lake Charles who innocently asked an African American woman about the size of her family and her religion. She became so upset and suspicious about his line of questioning that she "began to shout hysterically and finally collapsed. The scared agent fled to a negro cabin, which was soon surrounded by a mob of more than a hundred angry negroes. He was rescued by the police."

The stories that were circulating about attempted home invasions in Lafayette led to a mass meeting of more than 150 black citizens at the Good Hope Baptist Church. They adopted several resolutions, according to the *Lafayette Advertiser*, "pledging to furnish the authorities and officers with any information we have that would lead to the ferreting out of these crimes and to be used in any capacity by the authorities and officers of the city in helping them bring about the desired results in references to the crimes committed in Lafayette, Rayne, Crowley, and Lake Charles."

The meeting inspired a gathering in Lake Charles of "colored ministers, teachers, doctors, and businessmen" at St. Paul's A.M.E. Church. These civic leaders had met with the authorities about ways they could help to capture the killers that were wreaking havoc across the state. The meeting was presided over by Reverend Clarke, who, like many of the others, had spoken out publicly about the crimes and the fear in the black community.

The meeting was written about in the *Lake Charles Daily American-Press* by reporter E.H. Hamilton, who added his own thoughts about the murders:

Whereas we appreciate the efforts of our own officers and of those cities where the crimes have been committed, to protect their colored citizens against these blood-thirsty demons and bring the perpetrators to justice, we therefore feel there out to be some demonstration on our part to assist them.

Whereas the ax-man has paralyzed the domestic, industrial, social, and religious life among the negroes here and in those sections where his viciousness has been displayed, we therefore solicit funds from every race lover, peace preserver, and law abiding colored citizen of Lake Charles to assist in arresting this maniac.

Hamilton - along with other writers - referred to the Axman as "blood-thirsty demons" in the plural, not the singular. The idea of there being a conspiracy of killers was rampant in Louisiana - and it wasn't completely wrong. The Axman was a singular "blood-thirsty demon," but two of the murders had been committed by someone else, and they were likely not working alone.

If anything, the confusion about what was going on made things even more frightening and further increased the panic and dread that had permeated the region.

And that panic soon spread west to Texas.

10. "AX FIEND AT BEAUMONT"

BEAUMONT, TEXAS – FEBRUARY 19, 1912

The Axman was back riding the rails again after the Broussard murders. A month later he struck again, this time in the Texas town of Beaumont, which is only 60 miles west of Lake Charles.

Beaumont officially became a town in 1838, growing out of a settlement that had started on the west bank of the Neches River about a dozen years before. It began as a community of farmers and cattlemen but soon attracted merchants, banks, and hotel owners as it became a successful regional shipping center. By the 1880s, its location on the river put it in a position to ship lumber across the country and it became home to the first commercial rice mill in Texas. By the early twentieth century, the town was being served by the Southern Pacific; Kansas City Southern; Atchison, Topeka, and Santa Fe; and Missouri Pacific railroad lines.

Oil was discovered at nearby Spindletop Hill on January 10, 1901. The first well, the Lucas Gusher, exploded that day and shot oil hundreds of feet into the air. The explosion was so intense that the column was still gushing nearly 200 feet high nine days later. Beaumont now had the first major oil field in American history.

Within days of the discovery more than 40,000 curious tourists, speculators, and jobseekers had flocked to Beaumont. Restaurants, hotels, and stores were swamped as the city's population grew from 9,000 to 30,000 in just three months.

It was in this boom time for Beaumont that the Axman came to the city. I'm sure he'd been there before because, as mentioned earlier, I believe that he worked on the railroad, and Beaumont was a hub for four different rail lines in the early 1900s. For whatever reason, he decided that this time was when he was going to commit murder. Why? We will never know but perhaps it was for a reason as simple as having a weekend free from work. The slayings took place on a Sunday night.

The banality of a man committing murder in his free time is perhaps even more terrifying than the idea that he planned it months in advance.

This time, the Axman's victims were 30-year-old Hattie Dove; her son, Ernest, age 14; daughter Ethel, age 16; and her 18-year-old daughter Jessie Quirk, who was separated from her husband and had come to 1428 Cable Street to stay with her family. The home was located on the north side of the city - which was the "black section" - a block away from the Magnolia Avenue Baptist Church.

There was nearly a fifth victim in the crime. An unnamed black man also boarded with the family, but he worked at night, so he was out of the house when the killer arrived.

The Dove family had last been seen around 9:30 on Sunday evening, and the murders were discovered on Monday morning at 7:00 a.m. when a neighbor came to the house and discovered the carnage.

As with the other crime scenes, blood was found sprayed on the walls and soaking through the sheets on the bed. There was no sign of a struggle, leading the police to believe they had also been killed in their sleep. The ax had been left behind at the scene, propped against the wall. Blood remained on the blunt side of the head. Next to the ax was a cloth that the Axman had used to wipe the blood from his hands.

The ax turned out to be one of the oddities of the crime. It did not belong to the Dove family. Every household of this era had an ax. Families depended on wood to heat their homes and cook their meals. The Doves had an ax, but it had been left untouched. Strangely, the ax that had killed the family had come from the woodpile of a man who lived about two blocks away. Apparently, the killer had picked it up as he was walking to the Dove home. Even stranger? He left another ax in the man's woodpile to replace the ax that he'd taken with him. This anomaly has, of course, never been explained, but it was the first time that the Axman had done anything like this.

The newspaper coverage of the murders was just as lurid as in other cities, counting the number of the Axman's victims - as well as those committed by others - and describing the terror that was being experienced in the black community.

The *Beaumont Enterprise* reported:

Several arrests have been made in each case but so far there have been no convictions.

In the meantime, the negro quarters of the town where the murders are committed are in a state of siege. Negroes have forgotten what it is to sleep and keep vigil all night. They are prepared for trouble, too, and only a few nights ago, a negro woman, hearing a noise at her front door, shot through the panel without taking the trouble to inquire what she was shooting at. The position of the negroes is serious, however. Naturally superstitious and having nothing else to which to attribute the outrages, many of them are assigning supernatural causes, while all are so wrought up it is difficult to get an intelligent word out of them.

But not everything that appeared in the article about the most recent murders was racist and sensational. Whoever wrote the piece made one stunning announcement that rejected the ideas of those who believed that some sort of religious conspiracy was taking place:

The similarity of the elemental circumstances leaves no doubt but that all the murders were committed by the same person and that there is some eccentric motive for his crimes.

The Axman - the real killer, not the perpetrators of the crimes that looked like his - was one person. He was the "Ax Fiend," as some papers called him, and he was not finished with his bloody work.

The *Beaumont Enterprise* reported that "thousands and thousands of Negroes" (unlikely) filed past the bodies of the Dove family while they were lying in the morgue. They "sent fervent supplications to heaven" to be spared a visitation of this awful vengeance upon themselves. Many of the "wild-eyed spectators" were reported to moan that the "Lord had deserted them," and some allegedly cried that "a curse had fallen upon the race." It was Jim Crow-era Texas, and this was how white newspapers - and most citizens -- regarded the African Americans in those days. Before it was all over it was going to get a lot worse.

After the murders of the Dove family hardware stores in Beaumont began running out of locks, hasps, shotguns, and pistols. The black residents were arming themselves, which undoubtedly wasn't making the white citizens very happy.

The police rounded up the usual suspects and detained them, but all were eventually released. Soon after a mass meeting of concerned black citizens was held, and they raised a reward of $500 for the arrest and conviction of the killer. Tensions ran high and families began staying together, remaining awake in shifts to watch for any sign that the Axman might come to call. Talk circulated in the black community about armed guards that could be placed outside of homes or on the streets at night. The problem was - who knew when the killer might strike next?

"Frenzied with fright and excitement," black residents began to treat strangers - black or white - with suspicion, and many were forced to leave town because of fears that these strangers might be the "Ax fiend."

Unfortunately, the paranoia and fear resulted in a number of unintentional tragedies following the murders.

Horace Alexander, a 21-year-old married man, was standing watch at the home of his friend Adam Bobinaux in Beaumont while the two men's families slept inside. At some point in the night, Bobinaux mistook Alexander for the Axman and shot him, killing his friend instantly.

Max Warren, a young boy who suffered from sleepwalking, was accidentally shot by his neighbor in Smithville, Texas. West Duval, who was guarding his home against the Axman, saw the boy in the darkness and killed him.

In Gonzales, Texas rumors spread in the black community that a "strange Negro woman missionary" was in town - and she was part of the Church of the Sacrifice. The woman - whoever she was - was forced to leave town.

While trouble was stirring in Texas, people were still terrified in Louisiana. The town of Lake Charles had been deluged with "hoodoo doctors" who were selling charms to ward off the Axman.

Mounted patrol officer Ira E. Barker from the Lake Charles Police Department shot and killed a "hoodoo doctor" and lightning rod salesman named A.E. Johnson from Opelousas. Barker had tried to question the drunk and belligerent Johnson and then shot the man three times. Johnson had been selling lightning rods to help his black customers ward off evil spirits. One newspaper opined that perhaps all the murders were simply a conspiracy arranged by Voodoo doctors to help them sell charms.

No one took that suggestion very seriously.

A week later in Lake Charles, a black preacher named J.F. Anderson was arrested and sentenced to spend 30 days in jail for selling charms and powders. He claimed that they would "ward off diseases of all kinds" and "make the purchasers immune from visits from the Axman." He had simply been selling them, he told police, to "destroy all fears and dangers originating from the horrible murders."

It didn't work.

Another strange rumor that came to life in Lake Charles after the Dove murders encouraged black residents to use wet rags to seal their doors and windows. The rags were meant to prevent "fumes" from getting into their houses. The rumor claimed that the Axman had been spraying chloroform into his victims' homes, which explained why none of the families woke up when he butchered them. That was why, the story went, the back doors of the murdered families were always left open so that any trace of the chemical would be gone and would go undetected by the police. As far as wild stories went, this one actually made some sense, but there was no evidence that this was anything other than a rumor.

But rumors were the only news that many members of the black community could count on at the time. The newspapers were creating stories out of thin air, repeating the Axman's body count, and presenting African Americans as superstitious fools who were jumping at every shadow.

That was bad enough, but it soon got worse - and became even wilder and more misleading. An enterprising editor at the *El Paso Gazette* decided that by combining racism and black magic he could make the story of the repeat killings even spookier - and sell more papers. And what could be scarier in the Jim Crow South than Voodoo, black magic, and human sacrifice? Surely, it was implied, no white men could be involved in such heinous crimes, so it must be part of some sort of African American ritual.

The stories that followed guaranteed to sell papers to white readers. They were sensational, ridiculous, and inherently racist. And most of all they guaranteed that the story of a murder spree that involved only African Americans in the early 1900s would be never be taken seriously.

11. "VOODOO'S HORRORS BREAK OUT AGAIN"

The article appeared in the *El Paso Gazette* on March 14, 1912, with the headline "Voodoo Horrors Break Out Again." The story had a full-page to itself with two illustrations. On the left side of the page was a huge illustration of a small black child that was wrapped in the coils of a massive snake, describing how "Here all the horrors of Voodooism are revived, and little children go to their deaths a sacrifice to the serpent." The other illustration is a photograph of a group of African Americans with the caption, "A typical group of Louisiana rice pickers from whom the victims of the 'Sect of Sacrifice' are taken." But really, the tone of the article is captured in its unbelievable subtitle, which reads:

How the Cruel and Gruesome Murders of Africa's Wicked Serpent Worship Have Been Revived in Louisiana by a Fanatic "Sect of Sacrifice"

It's hard to know where to begin with a recounting of the article that probably fanned more racist flames than any other in the two-and-a-half-year saga of the "Mulatto Ax Murders." I have read a lot of blatantly racist material while researching this book, but I have to say this one is near the top of the list. I just need you to keep in mind that there is barely a shred of truth in the entire article.

The wildly inaccurate and unbelievably racist article that appeared in the El Paso Gazette, blaming "Voodoo cults" for the Axman murders that had been occurring across the region.

To start with, I want to stress that the murders had

nothing to do with Voodoo, which is a peaceful religious faith that was brought to Louisiana from Africa - via the Caribbean islands - by slaves, as early as 1719. Most of them came directly from West Africa, bringing with them their language and religious beliefs, which were rooted in spirit and ancestor worship. In the Fon language of West Africa, "Vodun" means spirit - an invisible and mysterious force that can intervene in human affairs.

Voodoo developed more prominently in Louisiana than in other parts of the new country, and one reason for that is largely because the French - then the Spanish, then the French again - colonized Louisiana. They were far more tolerant of the practices and the faiths of the slave population than were the British, who had come to America for religious freedom and then suppressed the faiths of anyone who didn't agree with them.

Another reason was the sheer number of slaves that were brought to Louisiana. According to the census of 1732, the ratio of slaves to French settlers was two to one. The white minority would have had a hard time suppressing the Voodoo faith, so they mostly didn't bother.

However, some worries popped up here and there. The first reference to Voodoo in official documents appeared in 1782 when the Spanish were in charge. In a document about imports to the colony, there is a terse line regarding black slaves from the island of Martinique. Governor Galvez wrote: "These Negroes are too much given to voodooism and make the lives of the citizens unsafe."

But I think the governor was less worried about Voodoo and more worried about rebellious slaves. A series of slave revolts had rocked Haiti and other islands in the Caribbean, and each time French colonists were driven from those lands and ended up in New Orleans. When they arrived, they brought their slaves with them - slaves who not only practiced Voodoo but who also may have been recently involved in uprisings.

Voodoo in Louisiana was a blend of different cultures. One of the most important cultures was Catholicism. Some people feel the people who practiced Voodoo started using Catholic saints, holy water, and the Lord's Prayer in their ceremonies as a way to hide Voodoo in plain sight. It's been suggested that slaves were forbidden to practice their religion, so they used Catholic saints and icons as stand-ins for important Voodoo deities.

But this may not be true. Some believe that it was a conscious decision to integrate Catholicism into Voodoo because the white man's magic did seem to have some power - you know since the white man had a better life as a slave owner than the people had as slaves.

For others, the blending of Voodoo and Catholicism was simply a natural course of events. After many years and generations away from their homeland, slaves slowly lost their old beliefs, and the predominant Catholicism of the French colony bled into their practices.

Voodoo in Louisiana grew to be quite a bit different than what was practiced in Haiti and other places. The evolution of the faith in the region created many new practices that most associate with some of the basics of Voodoo, including Voodoo dolls, gris-gris - which are small bags filled with magic items to bring good luck or protect the wearers of them from evil - and an assortment of magic charms and protections.

It was newspaper stories - no surprise there - that first created fear among white people about Voodoo. As early as

1817 sensational stories appeared in print about rituals, drums, "wild, uncontrolled orgies" and "serpent worship."

That's all going to seem very familiar a century later, as you'll soon see.

Voodoo worshippers were arrested on a regular basis, but usually, the charges were dropped - which turned out to be almost as bad as if they had been sent to jail. Rumors spread that Voodoo spells had either erased the evidence or clouded the minds of the judges and prosecutors. White residents feared that the religion - practiced by slaves and free people of color - was so powerful that it could entice followers to commit any crime or deed. Supernatural powers and secret drugs made Voodoo a force to be reckoned with. Slaves owners began to fear poison in their food. Men and women were convinced they could be forced to fall in love with anyone, just because of a sprinkle of magic powder. Even death could be held in check by the use of "zombie drugs."

As the years went by Voodoo fell out of fashion. The slaves were freed after the Civil War, Reconstruction came along, followed by the Jim Crow laws, which kept African Americans as second-class citizens for decades to come. Voodoo, by the early twentieth century, had become the stuff of pulp stories, folklore, and wild imaginations, but yes, it still had power. Voodoo frightened people - especially white people - who only saw the side of it portrayed in rumors, tall tales, and scary stories.

And what better time to resurrect those scary stories than when it could terrify both whites and blacks alike.

The *El Paso Gazette* reported, without hesitation, that the murders were all linked to "the horrors of Voodoo, with sacrifice of human life" and that it had been revived in the region by "fanatical negroes" leaving the authorities unable to

A group of African Americans identified as "rice pickers" in the article, from which the newspaper claimed the victims of the "Sect of Sacrifice" were taken

cope with the murders that had occurred as "rites of the Sacrifice Sect, as the new high priests of Voodooism are known." And, of course, what could the police do since many of the "victims have acquiesced in their slaughter." While that didn't make the tragedies any less horrible, the editor wrote:

It only emphasizes the intense fanaticism of the benighted Voodoo worshippers. This outbreak is regarded as the worst in the whole history of Voodooism. Never before has the cult obtained such a hold upon its followers or provoked them to more excesses than in the present instance.

For twenty years or more, Voodooism has been practiced in the United States in the mildest sort of way. The older negroes down here have always recognized and feared the power of Voodoo - the cult of the sacred serpent - but in recent years it has not led them to serious excesses.

However, the *Gazette* noted that this long period of calm had apparently served to increase the susceptibility of those "to who the mystic cult naturally appeals" - which was code for "black people," you know, all the "superstitious" people that the newspapers had been complaining about during the course of the murders. The past two decades had turned the "smoldering embers of fanaticism" into a flame that was now "burning with a fierceness never before equaled."

The writer must have been "researching" - and we'll use that term lightly - his story for a few weeks because he noted that the "latest outrage" had been the murders in Lake Charles, not the murders in Beaumont. He wrote in glowing terms about Felix Broussard - the "good type of Negro" - and his family and the discovery of their bodies after the murders. There was a note about the ax being found under Felix and Matilda's bed, and the bucket that was found next to the children's bed, which investigators believed was used to collect their blood.

After that, the editor goes off into the world of fantasy and imagination. He wrote:

Perhaps the strangest feature of this tragedy was the fact that the fingers of each hand of the victims were stretched apart by the murderers, those of the children being wedged open with paper and fastened with pins! The significance of this discovery became more apparent when it was found that above the door of the Broussard house the words 'Human Five' had been inscribed, and suggests that the Sacrifice Sect shared the belief in the mysticism of the figure five which has always been held by primitive people.

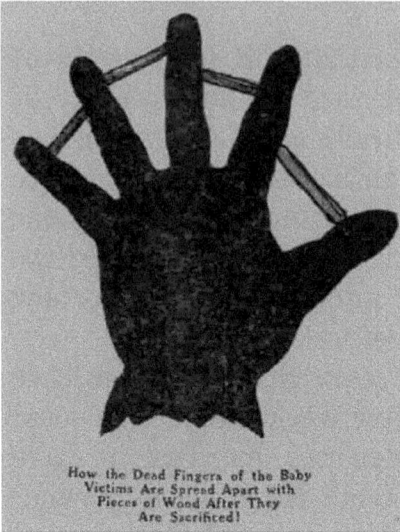

How the Dead Fingers of the Baby
Victims Are Spread Apart with
Pieces of Wood After They
Are Sacrificed!

A newspaper illustration used to illustrate how the hands of the Broussard family were displayed to represent the "Human 5." It's a nice illustration, but this never happened.

This is a tough one because, again, I'm not sure where to start with this. First, I suppose it should be mentioned (again) that there was nothing reported about the victims' hands at the crime scene. The fingers were not opened, the hands were not marked in any way, and the hands of the children were definitely not held in place by pins. So, we can debunk that altogether.

I was curious, though, about the "mysticism of the figure five" that the writer noted, because I do believe that the Axman did inscribe those words on the wall - it's just that he didn't do anything with the bodies to coincide with whatever message he was trying to leave behind.

There are several pagan and religious references to the number five. In some traditions, five is equivalent to the four elements plus the spirit, which is considered the fifth element. It's also symbolic of the five human senses, the points of the pentagram, and in Christianity, the wounds of Christ. Five is sometimes considered a bit chaotic, as found in some interpretations of the Tarot, in which the five indicates struggle and conflict.

What did the Axman want to signify with his message? He also left a biblical verse inscribed on the door:

"When he maketh the inquisition for blood, he forgetteth not the cry of the humble."

Does the verse connect to any of those possible meanings behind the number five? Or the "Human 5?" Not that I can easily see, but then we are trying to figure out what was going through the head of a man who had killed a couple of dozen people for no apparent reason. I can live with the fact that we'll likely never understand his motivations because, terrifyingly, it all made perfect sense to him.

But on with the article, which brings us to my favorite part - another "factual" section that was easily debunked, even for readers in 1912. I'll let the writer introduce this "theory":

But even more marked evidence of the importance attached to this figure by the Voodooists lies in the fact that every case of human sacrifice perpetrated during the present outbreak, there seems to have been an effort to slay just five persons.

What?

The writer then goes on to list all of the earlier murders and even throws in the Randall murders (although he mistakenly calls them "Wexford") by saying that six people had been butchered, but that one of them was an infant who had probably not been born yet when the cult had planned its human sacrifices. "Five separate families, each evidently intended to have five victims."

If you're confused, don't worry, you should be. Even if we leave out the most recent murders - on the timeline of this article - in Beaumont, there had already been seven murders that had occurred. All these murders were mentioned frequently in other newspaper stories about the killing spree. And if you've been keeping count, then you know that only two of the murders had five victims involved. Here's the score as it stood, ending with the Broussard murders in Lake Charles:

Rayne, Louisiana - 4 victims
Crowley, Louisiana - 3 victims
Lafayette, Louisiana - 4 victims
San Antonio, Texas - 5 victims
Lafayette, Louisiana - 6 victims
Crowley, Louisiana - 4 victims
Lake Charles, Louisiana - 5 victims

And then there were four more people killed at Beaumont, raising the numbers higher, but certainly not in groups of five. This editor apparently needed an editor himself.

He went on to add that even though a cross appeared on the churches attended by the "Voodoo worshippers," it was not there because of its Christian significance but because, with its four points and center, it "symbolizes the fateful figure five."

He was not even close to being finished with his "knowledgeable" diatribe against Voodoo and African Americans, though. The rest of the article was designed to create as large of a racial divide as possible in the region and to frighten everyone, black and white.

At regular services conducted at these churches, the rites celebrated are of the most weird character and involve considerable shouting and frenzied declamation, but, obviously, the sacrifice of human flesh is reserved for celebrations of a less public nature.

Voodooism, or Voodoo, as it is more properly though less commonly referred to, is based upon the worship of the snake god, represented at the rites of the sect by a live python or other large serpent. In Africa, where the cult originated, the serpent is held sacred and human sacrifices are constantly offered to him.

The writer continued, describing Voodoo ceremonies that he had undoubtedly never attended. If I had to guess I would say that most of his information about Voodoo came from the travel writings of Lafcadio Hearn, a quiet, scrawny, bug-eyed, weak-chinned, bird-legged writer who moved from Cincinnati to New Orleans in 1877. He spent the next 10 years in New Orleans, writing pieces about the city for national magazines like *Scribner's* and *Harper's Weekly.* His articles created the popular reputation of New Orleans as a place that was more like Europe or the Caribbean than like the rest of the United States. Essentially, he put the city of New Orleans on the tourist map.

His most popular articles were about Voodoo, and while wildly inaccurate he made the ceremonies that he witnessed - the phony ones dramatized for the tourist trade -- seem like something every adventurous traveler of the nineteenth century should see. Most of his articles portrayed voodoo rituals as snake handling, bourbon drinking, nude dancing, chicken killing affairs that ended with people sticking pins into dolls.

It's the reputation that Voodoo had endured for decades and one that undoubtedly added to the tall tales cooked up in the *El Paso Gazette.*

He described how Voodoo ceremonies began with a "bath of goat's blood," and then the "sacred serpent" would be brought out in a cage. He stressed that there was "no limit to the excess in which these fanatics indulge at their orgies."

A worshipper that receives "holy recognition" would stand on a box and the snake would wind around their bodies to the delight of the crowd. The spectators would "gaze with awe and feel that the candidate is really receiving divine power."

After this part of the ceremony, he wrote, "atrocious vows are made, and the final compact with Voodoo is ratified" - I don't even know what that means - and then "worshippers drink blood from a vase."

After the blood-drinking, naturally, the orgies begin. Between dances, white rum mixed with blood is served to the "frenzied dancing multitude, and in a few moments, pandemonium reigns." The dancers then "tear off their clothing, bite, scratch, and mutilate. Drinking and dancing continue until the participants fall about the arena senseless from exhaustion."

Before they start killing people - or the "goats without horns" - they killed a white chicken and a white goat and drink their blood. After that, they bring in the human sacrifice - which, of course, is a little white girl.

She is bound hand and foot and hung from a rope, and "then at a signal up goes the child and off falls its head at a single blow from a machete wielded by a young negro fanatic."

The writer then ends this bit of sensationalist, irresponsible "journalism" with one last swipe at how worthless the lives of African Americans were considered in Texas and Louisiana in 1912:

In the rice belt here, the life of the Negro is held rather cheap, but nevertheless, the authorities are determined to stamp out this fresh outbreak of Voodooism before it becomes so deeply rooted that it will defy their efforts.

In other words, we don't want the "Negroes" to start thinking they can start killing white people, too.

Unbelievable.

As ridiculous as this article - and others like it - seem to us now, there was no question that fear was continuing to spread. A story began circulating in Galveston, Texas in early March that the Axman "had posted notices that his toll in Galveston would be 'twenty-three Negroes'" and, as a result, the panic was wild. The *Houston Post* reported that extra police officers had to be called to duty from the reserve list "to stay at the station and answer telephone calls as well as assure frightened dusky callers that they would receive attention."

The *Press*, feeling slightly bemused and undoubtedly safe from a series of murders that only struck the black population, ran a skeptical article about the way African Americans in the Chenevert neighborhood of Houston were responding to the crisis:

Darkies are Panicky.
Report that Mysterious Axman is in Houston Causes Those of Chenevert District Sleepless Nights

Midnight oil, mysterious pans of cold water, uncanny exorcisms, knotted horse tails and too many other forms of incantations known to darky necromancy are playing part in a panicky epidemic through the Chenevert neighborhood.

This sudden oscillatory, seismic disturbance in the peace of mind of the colored population of Chenevert Street had its origins in a rumor, from some source that has not been run to its lair, that the author of the recent negro family massacres around Beaumont and Lake Charles had come to Houston and is now stalking the night in the Chenevert neighborhood.

In hope of keeping this mysterious and sinister being, man or devil, or whatever he or it is, away from their houses, the whole population is reported to have resorted to methods of the description alluded to above. Oil torches are left burning in their rooms all night, pans of water are placed on the floor and elsewhere about the room for the purpose of absorbing any portion of the evil influence that may happen to be hydrophobic, and other prestidigitations are performed carefully and throughout before retiring, in hope that those thus doing may be immune when the monster passes.

In order to supply the increased demand of oil growing out of the large consumption for this purpose, some of the Chenevert grocery and supply dealers on Chenevert Street found it necessary yesterday to lay in extra quantities of kerosene, while the pan demand took on proportions of a small flurry.

The Chenevert negroes have applied the name "Jack the Ripper" to the otherwise unidentified axman whose alleged presence in their midst is spreading terror. That some sinister joker is perpetrating one of the superstitious darkies of that side of town seems evident.

But the newspaper couldn't have been more wrong. There was no one playing a joke on the "superstitious darkies." The Axman was real, and he soon struck again.

He bypassed Houston, though, and the next murders occurred in a small railroad town outside of Columbus, Texas called Glidden.

12. "SIX MORE KILLED BY 'THE AXE-MAN'"

GLIDDEN, TEXAS – MARCH 26, 1912

The bodies were discovered just after daybreak. Parthenia Monroe, the grown daughter of Ellen Monroe, walked over to her mother's house early that morning. Parthenia lived with a grandmother just a short distance away. As she usually did, Parthenia opened the back door and walked into the house. Moments later she discovered her mother, four of her siblings, and a boarder who stayed with them had all been murdered in their beds.

The tiny community of Glidden was never meant to be much more than a railroad maintenance yard between Houston and El Paso. Located on the main rail line of the Southern Pacific Railroad, the townsite was originally established in 1885. The post office opened three years later, and the town flourished for a few years with a population that was never more than about 400 people. There were a few stores, some businesses, and three saloons to make sure the railroad workers never went thirsty.

Glidden became essential to war efforts starting with the Spanish-American War and continuing through the two world wars. Shortly after that railroads switched from steam engines to diesel and electric and the maintenance shops in Glidden became obsolete. The town faded away as the golden

In the railroad yards in Glidden in the early 1900s

age of railroading vanished. There aren't many people left in Glidden today, but in 1912 it was still a flourishing town, and it's no surprise that it became a stopping point for a killer who traveled by rail.

The Glidden victims were Ellen Monroe, age 46, a "black negress" as the newspapers described her, who was the wife of John Monroe. The couple was separated, and John was living in Yoakum at the time of the murders. Together the two had 14 children, four of whom were still living with Ellen at home. They were also killed by the Axman and included Alberta, age 8; Jessie, age 11; Dewey, age 12; and Willie, age 16.

Ellen also provided a room for a boarder named Lyle Finucane, age 37, an "octoroon of considerable intelligence" who worked for the Galveston, Harrisburg, and San Antonio Railroad, which had a yard in Glidden. The newspapers stated that he was married several years ago "to a girl of bright color and prepossessing appearance but separated from her two years ago." Since that time, he had been living at the Monroe house.

Once again, we have no idea how the Axman chose his victims. I think it's safe to surmise that he traveled - or worked for - the railroads and that this was his method for getting around the region, but how he chose the families that he wanted to kill remains a mystery which the killer took to his grave. However, it seems like a very large coincidence that Lyle Finucane also worked for the railroad. Was it possible that the Axman had encountered him through his job, knew about his family life, and followed him home to kill them all? It's certainly worth considering.

Also, based on the Axman's constant proximity to the railroad, as well as Glidden's importance to the railroads at that time, the small town was almost destined to become one of the killer's crime scenes.

And on March 26, it happened.

Parthenia Monroe discovered the bodies the following morning and alerted the authorities who quickly arrived on the scene. They determined that all the victims had been struck while they were sleeping. Lyle and Ellen were found in one bedroom, and the four children were in another. The oldest boy, Willie, had been sleeping in a cot, and the three other children were in the bed. All their skulls had been crushed with the blunt side of an ax that the sheriff determined had been taken from the family's own woodpile. It was, of course, left behind at the scene. Nothing had been taken from the house. The Axman, for all his other faults, was apparently not a thief.

Sheriff Bruce Mayes of Colorado County, who was based in nearby Columbus, told reporters that he believed the killer had entered through the back door of the house after

Neighbors gather around the Monroe House in Glidden in the wake of the murders (Courtesy Nesbitt Memorial Library)

picking up the ax. As he walked down the rear hall, he approached the bed in the east room and killed Lyle Finucane. Lyle's head was crushed in and "beaten away from the crown to the nose." He died instantly from the blow but fell from the bed to the floor, where his corpse was found.

Before Ellen awoke, or before she could get out of bed, she was struck in the head just over the right ear. Somehow, she made her way almost to the middle of the room and collapsed on the floor at the foot of the bed. She died there in a pool of her own blood.

Crossing the hall to the west room, the Axman crushed in the skulls of the three children in the bed - Alberta, Jessie, and Dewey. He then completed the killing by stepping to the cot in the southwest corner of the room and "braining" Willie, who lay face down with the right side of his face exposed.

None of the children showed signs that they had struggled or awakened. They were found in their beds in the positions that they were likely sleeping.

After the murders, the Axman returned to the back of the house and washed his hands in a tin wash pan before going back out of the door by which he'd entered.

The dead were discovered a few hours later, and by then the Axman was far away from Glidden.

The newspapers did all they could to continue to fan the flames of terror in the region. The *New Orleans Item* wrote:

From all that can be learned about the tragedy, the object was not robbery, but the murderer was either moved by the desire to kill for the sheer brutality of murdering or because he was moved by some fanatical belief that has caused the Louisiana authorities to attribute the murders in that state to the "Church of the Sacrifice."

This whole section is terror stricken by the new murders. The colored population has been to some extent aroused since the latest of the killings in Beaumont, but there has been no genuine fear that the axe-man would visit this town. The fear of the blacks is further increased this afternoon by the receipt of an unsigned letter declaring that the murder is to 'be repeated in this section tonight.' Negroes by the score are on their guard, armed against any intruder, while many other families had fled to Columbus."

The day after the murders five wagons carried six coffins to be buried at the Rocky Chapel Cemetery, and nine blacks were "held under arrest, believed to have knowledge of the crime," the *Houston Post* said, "although Justice of the

Peace Gregory waited until after the burial of the victims before taking further testimony."

One of the men arrested was Jim Fields, who came to the sheriff's attention when he followed a trail that led from the back door of the Monroe home to the house where Fields was staying. After footprints were found in the backyard Sheriff Mayes put out a call for bloodhounds, and the dogs sniffed out the trail. There was no other evidence to tie him to the killings, but since the bloodhounds led the police to his door - and he was black - he became a likely suspect.

What happened next convinced the authorities that they had found the killer - but they were wrong.

Fields no longer lived in Glidden. But he was briefly back in town, staying at the home of his brother. On March 6, 1912, he had married a woman named Ida Booker and had brought her to Glidden to stay with her mother while he sought work at a place called Buckholts, just outside of Colorado County. He got the job and had returned to Glidden to fetch Ida on March 26. He was supposed to report to work with his new employer the following day. On the evening before the murders, Fields had purchased two railroad tickets from the depot for Flatonia, Texas where he and Ida planned to live.

This raised even more suspicion about Fields - it looked like he planned to flee the area - so he and his wife were both arrested.

The sheriff was sure he had the right man. First, there were the bloodhounds, then the train tickets to leave town, plus Fields had $30 in cash on him, which was an "exorbitant amount of money for a black man to be carrying around." Some rumors claimed Fields had a jacket with blood on it and that his shoes were taken to the crime scene and they matched the footprints found behind the house. However, neither of those things turned out to be true.

A few days later, after hearing testimony about things Ida allegedly said to her former landlord, C.M. Bailet, Justice of the Peace Aubrey Gregory decided that Fields must be guilty of murder. According to this second-hand witness -- this would have been dismissed as hearsay at trial -- Ida had told him that her new husband had acted very suspiciously after the Monroe murders. This was the story that Bailey claimed Ida had told him:

On the night of March 26, we were at Charlie Fields' house, waiting for the train to go to Flatonia. About 12 o'clock we started to the train in a wagon, with Charlie Fields and his wife, for Glidden. They were taking us to the early morning train No. 9.

When we reached Glidden, we found out the night train would not stop, so we left our trunk in the depot and started back home with Charlie and his wife. When we came to a house, I asked Jim who lived there and he told me this is the house where Lyle Finucane and Ellen Monroe live. Then Jim said that we would get out, he and I, and the others would go on. We took our grips with us. After we were out of the wagon, I asked Jim what we were going to do and he asked, "Will you stand by me in anything?" I told him that I would as long as it was right. Jim said, "Come on then."

We went to the front gate. I stood by the post and Jim went around to the back of the house. From where I was, I could not see Jim go in the back door. He was gone about twenty minutes and during that time I heard something that sounded like licks. When Jim came out of the house, I asked him what he was doing and he said that I wanted to know

everything. We then went over to a house nearby to leave our
grips. After we left the house, Jim asked me again if I would
stand by him in everything, and I told him that I would so
long as it was right.

After this dramatic presentation of "evidence," Ida
Fields was released on bail, and Jim was held as the murderer
of Lyle Finucane and the Monroes. This news caused an
uproar in Glidden's black community. Even though the
murders were considered to be the next in a line of identical
murders of slaughtered families, the locals were terrified by
the fact that the Axman might be someone they knew, with
relatives right there in town.

But while Jim was in jail the murders continued.

That wasn't enough to prevent the authorities from
putting him on trial, though. Jim was indicted for the murders
in Glidden on May 17, 1912. On that day he met his legal
counsel for the first time since he had been arrested a month
and a half earlier. He had two attorneys to represent him -
Chris Grobe and Gus Miller. The biggest issue in their defense
didn't seem to be trying to show that Fields was not a killer.
They were having problems coming up for a reason as to why
Jim had $30 in his pocket. They were seeking witnesses who
could explain how he came into so much money.

The trial began on May 20. Chris Grobe was seriously
ill and didn't attend. Perhaps worse, Gus Miller admitted to his
client that this was only his second trial. Luckily, another
attorney, Charles K. Quin, was appointed to his case.

On the second day of trial, Grobe returned to court, and
a couch was brought in for him to lie down on because he was
too dizzy to sit up for an extended amount of time. During
the proceedings, the attorney reclined on the couch as he

listened to testimony and asked questions of the witnesses. In Fields' defense, several upstanding members of the white community appeared on his behalf and testified that he was a man of good character. The statement that had allegedly come from Ida, through her old landlord, was never admitted at the trial.

On May 27, the case against Jim Fields went to the jury, and they quickly returned with a verdict of "not guilty." It was reported that many of the onlookers in the courtroom cheered when the verdict was returned.

One down and five to go - the prosecution intended to try Fields for all the Glidden murders, one at a time. It took until September 23 but all charges against Fields were finally dismissed. He was released from jail and no one else was ever arrested for the murders in Glidden.

Jim and Ida Fields never lived together after the trial. In 1915 Ida filed for divorce on the grounds that Jim had deserted her on March 27, 1912 - the day he had been arrested for the murders.

More tragic was the fact that while Jim was in jail and being put on trial for killing the Monroes, the Axman was still seeking victims in Texas.

On April 12, he had struck again.

And it's possible that these murders occurred so soon after the attack in Glidden because the Axman needed to prove that he was still out there and that if he wanted to take a life no one could stop him.

Why was he worried that he wouldn't get credit for his gruesome work? Because in early April - soon after the murders in Glidden - someone else had confessed to his crimes.

Clementine Barnabet was back in the newspapers again.

13. "THE 'AXE-WOMAN'S' CONFESSION"

Clementine Barnabet had been in jail since being arrested by Sheriff LaCoste back in November 1911. He was convinced at the time that she had not acted alone and was intent on finding the rest of the "cult" who had killed the Randall family. He was right when he determined she had accomplices, but I don't think they were ever a cult called the "Church of the Sacrifice."

While Clementine was behind bars the murders continued. First, it was Marie Warner's family in Crowley, and then the Broussard murders in Lake Charles. As mentioned already, I do think Clementine knew about the Warner murders - at least she knew who committed them - but the Broussard murders were the work of the Axman.

It didn't matter as far as Clementine's confession went, though; the murders had been in all the newspapers, and it was easy for her to cook up a story that tied them all together. The authorities would later refer to the young woman as "demented," and I'm afraid they were right.

On April 1, 1912, Clementine confessed to everything. Branded as the "Axe-Woman," she maintained that she had not been working alone in what she called her "midnight assassinations." With no apparent remorse for her crimes, she told the police about her many victims - never explaining how the murders had continued while she was in jail.

SHE MURDERED 17

CLEMENTINE BARNABET.
The woman under indictment at Lafayette, La., charged with slaying several families, numbering seventeen persons. She has made a detailed confession, and says her actions were inspired by a strange desire to press to her bosom the bodies of murdered infants, which action gave her intense satisfaction. She names two other women, who, she says, assisted in her crimes for the same reasons. The Barnabet woman is a member of the Church of God, the so-called sacrifice sect.

She did have accomplices, she claimed but refused to give up their names. She did say that her "ax gang" consisted of two black men and three black women, including herself. Of course, this news led to speculation that they had been the "Human 5" killers.

To understand the entirety of Clementine's very strange statement and confession, I have combined the information that she gave to the authorities with an interview that she did with a reporter named R.H. Broussard from the *New Orleans Item*. During her time in jail, she had full access to the press, even during her trial. Her story was making headlines - even after officials decided that most of it was untrue and that she was a "lunatic."

My name is Clementine Barnabet. I was born and partly raised near the town of St. Martinville and moved to

Lafayette about three years ago when I began to lead a life of degradation. I have never been married. It was while in the company of two other women and two men, while in New Iberia, that we met an old Negro who told us he could sell us "candjas" with which he could do as we pleased and we would never be detected and would be protected from the hands of the law by the mere fact of these "candjas" being in our possession. We bought them, and paid $3 each for them and left New Iberia the same night, returning to Lafayette, when we began to plan our actions. We had not yet decided on committing any murders, but it was while we were discussing our future plans that the question came up as to whether we could kill and be protected by the hoodoos.

One of the gang was instructed to go to New Iberia and interview the hoodoo man, who said we were safe in any and all actions which we might do. Our lives would at all times be fully protected by the power of the hoodoos."

The murders had started in Rayne. They drew lots, after deciding to put that family to death. The short straw fell to Clementine, who lived in Rayne next to the railroad depot. Disguised as a man she secured an ax, entered the house, and brained the mother and her children. She left behind the man's clothing that she had worn and then returned to her sister's house. She boarded the midnight train and returned to Lafayette without anyone noticing her.

Her arrival back in Lafayette proved to the gang that she had been protected by the power of the hoodoo "candjas."

When the killers moved on to Crowley, Clementine and the two other women broke into the house. The others watched while Clementine committed the murders. After explaining how she had killed the mother and father, both in one bed, she said, "It was an easy matter to get rid of the two small children. We thought it was better to kill them than to leave orphans, as they would suffer."

She told the reporter, "We never spoke of committing any more murders until some time in February. The night before an election we knew that all the officers would be busy 'politicking,' so we went to the refinery and there we laid our plans, not knowing who would be the victim or victims."

She told the authorities that the murdered families had not been pre-selected by any kind of method. In her statement, she said, "These families were not selected particularly. We started out not knowing who the victims would be."

She said that they simply looked for a house where there was a light on so that they could see inside. There was no motive for the crimes, she claimed.

After killing the Andrus family, she explained: "We took the man and the woman, placed them in a kneeling position beside the bed, and left the house. I was one of the first to aid the relatives the next day and helped prepare the bodies for burial."

Clementine's confession continued with details about the murders in November 1911. In truth, these were the only killings that she could offer any details about because they were the only ones she was involved with.

At that time, she had been working for Mrs. Guidry in Lafayette, where she was employed as a live-in maid. Mrs. Guidry's house was about one block away from the Randall home. Clementine said that she left her house shortly before midnight to meet up with at least one other member of the "axe gang."

After killing Norbert Randall and his family, Clementine said that she encountered Reverend King

Harrison of the Sacrifice Church. Harrison was in town holding a revival meeting and she claimed that she warned Harrison - who was arrested and released after the Warner murders - to stay away from the home of Norbert Randall. She told the minister that she had just killed the entire family.

Clementine had gotten into the Randall house through the kitchen door at the rear of the house and had found the family asleep. She and her accomplice - although there was likely more than one - used a lamp to guide them through the dark house, but before doing so, they had stuffed rags into the keyholes on the front and back doors so that no light could be seen from outside. The detectives had noted this when they later investigated the scene.

Clementine described how she had killed Norbert Randal and his wife and then slaughtered their children with the blunt side of the ax. She claimed that one of the children tried to escape after being awakened by the noise, taking several steps before being felled by the ax.

After the murders, Clementine returned to the Guidry home. Her clothing, covered with blood and brains, were removed in the backyard. When she lifted the fastening rope on Mrs. Guidry's gate latch, she left behind a trace of blood that was later found by Sheriff LaCoste, leading to her arrest.

As she continued her grim tale, she openly bragged about seeing people converging on the Randall crime scene the next morning. She stood out in front of the house herself and laughed at the commotion she had created. It was this behavior that caught the attention of the sheriff and led to the discovery of her bloody clothes and her arrest.

After the chemist from New Orleans tested her clothing and it was found to be human, her fate was sealed as far as Sheriff LaCoste was concerned - at first anyway. He remained convinced that she had been involved in the Randall murders but beyond that, his faith in her story started to waver.

He was well aware that Clementine hadn't come up with her "confession" until she had been in jail for months. She had also retracted her testimony against her father, Raymond, and claimed that she had been responsible for the murders of the Andrus family, which she had accused him of committing. With no evidence other than some bloody clothes to link her to one crime scene, LaCoste - as well as other investigators and members of the press - began to grow skeptical of her story.

And that's when things started to get even crazier.

Soon after her confession began appearing in newspapers, Clementine started issuing warnings that other families would be murdered by "her friends." She announced that 13 other people were already decided upon as the next victims of the "Sacrifice Church." Even though no one else in the Lafayette area was killed, this was not as hollow of a threat as many officials thought. As I have mentioned already, I think that the Warners in Crowley *were* murdered by Clementine's accomplices in an attempt to shift blame away from her. It didn't work.

And there were more murders - but not in Louisiana. The Axman's final spree took place in Texas.

Meanwhile, the newspapers were wildly printing Clementine's confession, along with any other related stories they could find - or make up. The *Lake Charles Daily Times* reported that another "Sanctified" preacher had been questioned about the ax murders. It seemed that the Sanctified Sect of the Sacrifice Church was busy converting members of the black community in large numbers. The minister picked up by police was known only as "Thompson," and was said to have recruited many blacks to the "Sacrifice Sect" of some mysterious church. The news story claimed that after members joined the order they were "sanctified" and could no longer sin against God, no matter what crimes they committed. When asked by the authorities to name some of the new converts, his memory developed a lot of holes and he admitted that he knew none of their names.

On that same day, there was a report of a close encounter with the Axman in Algiers, just outside of New Orleans. A man named Howard Koppel arrived home shortly after midnight on a Sunday night "just in time to see a huge mulatto negro, armed with an ax, entering through a kitchen window." The "huge mulatto negro" had opened the window with a file and then raised the window to climb through, first removing his shoes.

According to Koppel, he had surprised the would-be killer. "I saw he carried an ax in his hand," he said. "I shouted at him and dashed upstairs to my room to get my revolver. The man in his haste ran into some supports for a vine and must have been knocked down, losing his hat and ax."

Koppel reportedly fired a shot at the fleeing figure, who was pursued by some neighbors before disappearing.

And then back to the Barnabet family and their many stories.

Clementine's brother, Zepherin, now had his own story to tell. He claimed that Clementine and a black man by the name of Mac Thomas, along with a woman who used the name "Duce," were involved in the killings together. Zepherin confirmed that the three of them had planned to go to New

Iberia to buy the Voodoo charms but had stayed in Lafayette to murder the Andrus family. But Zepherin was sure that his father had been involved, too.

The next morning Raymond had roused him from his sleep and demanded that his son go to the Andrus home - now a murder scene - and bring back the pipe that Raymond had left behind there. Needless to say, he refused.

At this point, after changing her testimony against her father for the Andrus murders, Clementine changed her story again and accused Raymond of not only killing that family but also committing the earlier massacres in Rayne and Crowley. She had now changed her mind about how many people she had killed and when asked about the changing number, she couldn't explain it. It was the same as when she was asked to reveal why the murders were committed in the first place. She refused to say - or perhaps she just couldn't make up a story that explained them.

The newspapers were still printing stories about her confession on their front pages, but even the reporters who had been writing lurid tales of Voodoo and cult sacrifices were starting to have a hard time believing what she was telling everyone. One noted, "Clementine's confession has been received with varying shades of belief owing to the positive way she swore in the trial of her father, and the misleading information she has given as to her accomplices."

The newspapers had created so much confusion in the case that it was almost impossible for investigators to understand what was going on. The public was becoming even more confused. Was there really a "Church of the Sacrifice," and if so, was it some sort of Voodoo cult?

No one knew.

Newspapers were still printings articles that stoked "Ax-Mania" in the region, though. It didn't even matter if they were true, or that another version of Clementine's story had replaced the version they were printing. They just wanted to keep the sensational story on the front page - no matter what it took.

One reporter stated that there had recently been two attempted break-ins in the same neighborhood in Lafayette where the Andrus and Randall families had lived, as well as possible sightings of the Axman. Sensational tales continued to spread about a "voodoo conspiracy."

Some stories reminded readers that when Clementine had first appeared in court after her initial arrest that she had rocked back and forth in the witness chair and let out "screams of hysterical laughter." Her eyes had rolled back in her head and she declared that the Randall family had been killed because "they had refused to obey church orders." She added that the Andrus family had also refused to "obey a message from God," which had been passed to them by a "Voodoo doctor." A reporter added that Clementine had been seen with this reported doctor and the other "religiously crazed Negro fanatics," who had gone into the Andrus house, hacked the family into pieces and ended their sacrifice with "weird prayers and incantations."

A Kentucky newspaper, the *Hartford Herald*, ran a story that put Clementine as the leader of the cult known as the "Church of Sacrifice," directing all the murders. It was said that she believed that by taking human life she and her followers would be able to obtain immortality. She was not afraid of being arrested, she said, "Because I carry a 'voodoo' which protected us all from punishment."

In this story, the "axe gang" had changed from a small group of five people to an entire cult, with as many women as men, all sharing in the killing. Clementine alluded to the fact that most of the murders occurred on nights when the blacks of the Sacrifice Church would have some sort of traveling revival in various communities. During the services, the followers would be worked up into a religious frenzy and then find a family that they wanted to slaughter. In a quote that Clementine likely never made, she said that once "heads and limbs were separated from torsos and strewn over the house," the rest of the congregation would arrive and begin some sort of "sacrificial ceremony."

The story went on to say that the authorities hoped to arrest at least 50 individuals involved with the cult and that Clementine was aiding in their investigation.

I don't think that it's necessary for me to rehash the crime scenes so that the reader can see how wild and inaccurate this article was. I think you can figure that out for yourself.

Arrests continued around Lafayette, thanks to Clementine's confession. One of those arrested was Joseph Thibodeaux, who Clementine claimed was the Voodoo doctor who had sold her and her "axe gang" the charms that were supposed to keep them safe as they committed crimes. She said that he also gave her the ideas for the crimes, but Thibodeaux swore that never happened. Not only that, but he also stated that he was certainly not a "Voodoo priest." He practiced root medicine and healing and a newspaper that came to his defense stated that he "has been regarded as peaceful in disposition and harmless in intention" and was "noted for the practice of conjuring warts away."

The police also arrested Clementine's half-sister, Pauline, and a woman named Valena Mabry. They were suspected of being two of the women in the "axe gang." Both denied any involvement in the crime and were released.

Soon after the confession, Sheriff LaCoste reported receiving a letter in the mail about the Axman murders. The writer claimed to be one of the "105," who were banded together to murder Negro families by an ax. The writer condemned the vile acts of murder, but he also confessed to taking part in them. He claimed that the victims were chosen in advance and "marked" by a man who came to town and made the necessary selections. After the victims were marked, "others" were dispatched to those towns to kill them.

The motive for the murders was a religious one. They were killed on authority given to the "105" by the "Sixth and Seventh Books of Moses." You won't find these books in the Bible. They are said to be "magical texts," allegedly written by Moses, which didn't surface until the nineteenth century.

The books are real, but whether or not they were written by Moses remains a mystery. The Sixth and Seventh Books of Moses contain symbols and spells used to instruct the Israelites about the "laws of magic." These "lost books of Moses" are different than the original five books of the Bible, which are attributed to him. They are considered a grimoire of ancient magic incantations, spells, and symbols and allegedly contain secret knowledge that could not be included in the Bible.

The Sixth and Seventh Books of Moses were traditionally published in one volume, first appearing in Pennsylvania in 1849. The book soon gained an evil reputation among the German population and those who were familiar with its lore. It was associated with "hexing" - or folk magic -

because the text provided instructions on how to conjure and control spirits and demons. It also contained spells and incantations that were beneficial to the user as well as spells that would duplicate some of the biblical plagues of Egypt, turn a staff into a serpent, and other miraculous happenings. Much of the volume was made up of reproduced symbols that were allegedly copied from old woodcuts. Some copies were printed, at least partially, with red ink. A few hand-copied editions were alleged to exist that had been written in blood.

The book eventually found an audience among those who practiced the West African conjuring known as "hoodoo." Readers may have noticed that many of the newspaper articles from the period that I quoted in this book use Voodoo and hoodoo interchangeably, but they are not the same thing. The problem was that most whites of that period didn't know the difference. This is why Joseph Thibeaux insisted that he was not a "Voodoo priest" but a root healer or hoodoo practitioner. The main difference between the two is that Voodoo is an actual religion, hoodoo is not. Voodoo has its own rituals, leaders, teachers, representatives, and services, plus two different branches - the Voodoo of New Orleans and Louisiana, and the Vodue of Haiti. Hoodoo, on the other hand, is not a religion and is practiced by individuals, sometimes called root doctors or root healers, who claim to have certain magical abilities and sell charms and potions. There's no question that it was an offshoot of Voodoo, but it's very different in practice. To whites, though, it was all scary, so it was easy to blend it into the mixture of the Axman murders and the mysterious "Church of the Sacrifice."

There is no indication as to whether Sheriff LaCoste took the letter seriously or if he dismissed it - as he should have - as the work of a crank.

But Sheriff LaCoste had a mess on his hands. It was becoming clear that Clementine was a lunatic. The public thought she was, and so did the newspapers. She'd changed her story many times, and even though she had offered the sheriff leads to find the other members of the so-called "Human 5" gang, the search resulted in a dead-end.

Even though hardly anyone believed her story by the time she was indicted, Clementine would go to trial. District Attorney Howard E. Bruner believed that some of the murders were copycat crimes, but he also believed that Clementine was a "moral pervert" who was capable of everything she confessed to, including the sexual caressing of the corpses of her victims. Apparently, that was enough to try her for murder. He officially filed charges against her on April 14, 1912.

A reporter from the *Weekly Town Talk* in Alexandria, Louisiana was one of the reporters who interviewed Clementine in her cell while the grand jury was deliberating whether to indict her for the Randall murders. She sang "Nearer My God to Thee" and talked freely with the newspapermen while smoking a cigar that one of the men had given her. She smiled while recounting yet another version of her "gruesome confession" and got "added gratification in the thought of her photograph appearing in the papers."

When she received the news that she had been indicted, she showed "no other emotion than the shrug of her shoulders."

While in jail waiting for her trial to start, Clementine confessed to a total of 35 murders. Every time that she re-told her story, though, the details changed, so it was impossible to know if anything she said was the truth.

Her defense attorneys claimed the 19-year-old young woman was insane - and they were probably right. However, Dr. E.M. Hummel of New Orleans, Dr. R.D. Voorhies, and Dr. John Tolson all reported that while Clementine was "morally depraved, ignorant, and of a low-grade of mentality," they did not discover any signs of insanity. After the reports from the doctors, she was pronounced sane enough to stand trial, which she did in October 1912.

The trial was fairly straightforward and focused on the Randall murders - likely the only ones she actually committed. The star witness was Dr. Metz, the chemist from New Orleans, who testified that the brain and blood samples from Clementine's clothing matched those of the Randall family.

Sheriff LaCoste, as well as other state's witnesses, testified that Clementine offered several variations of her story and that her confession lost credibility as proof of her lies were revealed in testimony from other witnesses. However, the biggest problem with Clementine's story was the fact that the murders continued to occur even after she was locked up. The prosecution moved quickly past that issue during the trial.

Instead, they asked the jury to focus on Clementine's odd behavior, as pointed out by her former employer, Mrs. Guidry. She said that Clementine was very light on her feet and would tread quietly as she carried out her housekeeping duties to sneak up on her employers. Clementine would then laugh out loud with some "perverse pleasure" after startling them with her undetected presence in the room. This was offered as evidence that she could have easily entered the home of the sleeping Randall family without awakening anyone.

Crowds filled the courtroom to see the woman that so many had been reading about in the newspapers. One paper, though, *The Times* from Shreveport, noted that no African Americans attended the trial. A *Times* reporter claimed, "Negroes fear that Clementine is possessed of the 'evil eye' and capable of casting a spell upon one and therefore none of her race are attending the trial."

On October 24, 1912, the case was sent to the jury, and they had completed their deliberations before noon - Clementine was found guilty of murder and sentenced to life at the Louisiana Penitentiary.

She attempted to escape in July 1913 but was caught the same day. Aside from that one incident she was a model prisoner but was not behind bars for long. According to one brief report, Clementine received a "procedure" that was said to have "restored her to normal condition," and she was released on good behavior after serving 10 years.

What became of her after that was unknown. The newspapers of the day had no interest in keeping track of a poor black woman who was released from prison, even one that had once been as notorious as Clementine Barnabet.

What part of Clementine's story was true, and what part was created from her imagination? And what part of it was nothing more than sensational fiction concocted by the newspapers? The story of her trial appeared in newspapers all over the country when it ended with one paper reporting that it was believed that 300 people had been slain by the "sacrifice sect" during the previous six years. The newspapers seemed to have as little need for the truth as Clementine did.

But there was solid evidence found against Clementine. The case didn't completely hinge on her confession. It's believed that she did commit at least one of the massacres - the Randall murders - but probably no others. It's impossible to know if any of the others were connected to her, although I believe that one of them was. But even then, we'll never know for sure. We can be fairly certain, however, that none of the murders had anything to do with a Voodoo cult or the alleged "Church of the Sacrifice."

In late March 1912, while Clementine Barnabet was safely behind bars in Lafayette, the Axman had murdered another family in Glidden, Texas. Although another man had been tried for the crime, Jim Fields was eventually cleared of any connection to the murders.

Strangely, according to the San Antonio Express, an unnamed attorney from Lake Charles had written a letter to Constable J.M. Everett of Columbus, "foretelling the tragedy at Glidden and predicting that the perpetrators would proceed to San Antonio, where another family was marked for slaughter."

This was odd, but there was another letter - this one mailed to the San Antonio City Marshal - dated April 2, 1912, that was even more chilling. It stated that "a crime identical with that of the Casaway atrocity would be committed in San Antonio on April 12." The letter was also said to have included "a description of a negro whose presence in various towns is coincident with these gruesome affairs."

It is unknown if the description that was provided matched any suspects in any of the murders, but the letter was right about one thing - the date of the Axman's next murder.

14. "AX MAN KILLS FIVE IN SAN ANTONIO"

SAN ANTONIO, TEXAS – APRIL 12, 1912

Early in the morning on April 12, a young black maid name Callie Burse walked over to the home of William Burton and his family on North Center Street in San Antonio. The house was located just east of the train station and only a few blocks from the home of the Casaway family, who had been murdered in their beds one year before.

It's very unlikely that this young woman was thinking about the Casaways as she walked to the Burton home. She had been paid to take over a can of kerosene, the repayment of a loan by a local preacher to William Burton, a 26-year-old porter who worked at Sommer's Garden, a popular saloon and bowling alley. William was described in the newspapers as a "sober and industrious negro, who had been employed for years in various saloons as a porter and stood high in the estimation of his employers." He had never been known to be in any kind of trouble and was well-liked in the community. No one could imagine why anyone would want to kill him, which made the events of April 12 ever more tragic.

When she reached the Burton home no one answered when she knocked on the door. It was just after 7:00 a.m., but most families were awake and busy by such an hour. Anxious to finish the job that she had been given, she walked around

House at 724 North College Street in which William Burton, his wife, two children and brother-in-law were murdered.

Newspaper photo of the scene outside of the Burton house in the aftermath of the murders

to a side window and peered inside. She was stunned to see that the curtains that covered the window were spattered with blood. Her scream attracted the attention of the neighbors, who notified the police.

Officials, including Bexar County Sheriff John Wallace Tobin, soon arrived on the scene and entered the house. Blood was everywhere. The walls, the ceiling, and the floors were streaked with it. They found signs that the killer had entered through the kitchen window at the back of the house.

The first body they discovered was that of William Burton's 20-year-old wife, Carrie. She was face down on the floor next to the bed. Her skull had been crushed by the blunt side of an ax and - in a new element to the crimes - a large knife was sticking out of her back. Several newspapers identified it as a butcher's knife.

William Burton's body was still on the bed. He was lying face down and his head had also been crushed. The *Houston Post* stated that the broken blade of a large pocketknife had been jammed into his back.

There was more carnage in an adjoining bedroom. The Burtons' two children, Naomi, age 3, and Edward, age 1, were found with their skulls crushed as well. Lying next to Edward on the blood-covered floor was Carrie's brother, Leon Evers. His head had also been smashed and a knife was also found protruding from his back. A bucket had been left in the children's bedroom and the water inside of it was stained a pinkish color by blood. The Axman had washed his hands there before he left the house.

The police officers were quick to recall the bloody crime scene left behind at the Casaway house, only a few blocks away. As with the Casaways, aside from the broken and bloody bodies of the victims, nothing had been touched in the house. Robbery was ruled out as the motive.

Carrie's mother, Betty Evers, later told the police that she had visited with her daughter, son, and the children around 8:00 p.m. the previous evening. William had returned home from work around midnight. Neighbors swore that William had no enemies, but the woman who lived next door to the Burtons reported that she had been awakened by her dog after the animal responded to some strange noises around 2:00 a.m. She, of course, thought little of it at the time, but her report helped the police to come up with an approximate time of death for the Burtons.

It was obvious to the police, the public, and the newspapers that the Axman had returned to San Antonio. Reporters immediately seized on the links between these new murders and the crimes that had occurred across Louisiana and Texas over the last two years.

The *Houston Post* was the first newspaper to suggest that these had been religious killings - not necessarily linked to the "Church of the Sacrifice" but to the fact that Carrie Burton had white blood. The reporter suggested that this could have been the motive. The article stated:

William Burton, the husband and father murdered today, was a pure blood negro, black as night. His wife was half white. Their two children showed the strong strain of white blood in their skin, but with negro hair and other characteristics.

Ten months ago, the Casaway family, father, mother, and three children, were killed with an axe close by the Burton cottage. The Casaway woman was half white. Her children showed the white strain as did the Burton kids.

Lizzie Casaway had been white, but the point was the newspaper suggested that because the families were of mixed race, that this could have been the reason they were killed. This led to the string of murders sometimes being referred to as the "Mulatto Ax Murders."

The newspapers may have suggested this idea first, but it's also possible that they got the idea from Sheriff Tobin, who was also working on the same angle. According to a statement released by his office, "the crime was the result of religious fanaticism. This belief is based upon the similarity of the condition in which the bodies of the victims were left in this tragedy and other mysterious murders which have occurred in South Texas and Louisiana." He was working under the assumption that the murders were "part of the religious propaganda of a secret sect" and the fact that Carrie, her brother, and her two children were of mixed race and that played a role in their murder.

This could have been part of the Axman's motivations - we'll never know for sure. "Mulatto" was a word not usually used by Louisiana and Texas newspapers at the time. It was more often found in out-of-state papers to describe someone of mixed race, but to people and newspapermen in the South, "blacks" were black, no matter what their skin tone. Even if a person had only a small amount of African American blood in their ancestry, they were still considered black.

But the significance of those of mixed race might be important in the story of the Axman. A case might be made that the Axman was a religious fanatic intent on killing light-skinned blacks or mixed-race families. Sherriff Tobin - as well as other lawmen and reporters - pointed to a biblical verse as the killer's possible motivation. It appears in the Book of Matthew:

And now also the axe is laid unto the root of the trees: every tree therefore which bringeth not forth good fruit is hewn down, and cast into the fire.

Could the Axman have started his deadly mission based on this passage? It's possible that he believed that the trees (people) that were bringing forth bad fruit (mixed-race children) needed to be "hewn down," as the Book of Matthew commanded. This might have been his own interpretation of the scriptures, or perhaps he heard it at one of the many revival meetings across the South and took the verse to heart.

There is no doubt that the Axman was an African American. Records show that the vast majority of serial killers are white, but there are exceptions. I believe the Axman was one of them. There is no way that he could have entered and escaped from the neighborhoods where he claimed his victims if he were white. He would have stood out and been remembered. White men simply did not go into those communities at the time, unless they were police officers or bill collectors, of course. Could the Axman have been trying to "purify" the black race by removing those who had white blood? It's certainly a theory worth considering.

In San Antonio in 1912, though, white police officers refused to believe that the misinterpretation of a Bible verse could be done by someone of the Christian faith. They put out a call to black residents to let the police know if they knew anything "about the practices of Voodooism."

They were still looking for members of the "Church of the Sacrifice," who many black residents in the community were convinced were in town. They were again living in a state of fear, standing guard outside their homes, and nailing their windows closed. Lights were left burning throughout the night, and dogs were brought into the house to raise the alarm over any intruders. Those who were of mixed race were even more terrified.

Sheriff Tobin told the *San Antonio Express*, "Possibly the fact that the Burton woman was fair-skinned may have been the incentive" for her murder. The killer might have believed he had been given a "literal command from the Most High to commit murder under certain conditions."

Terror was ratcheted up even higher when some members of the black community began receiving unsigned chain letters from Houston. They included a prayer that read,

"We implore thee to bless all mankind and keep us from all evil and take us to dwell with thee." Each letter was unsigned and included the instructions to "copy it nine times and send it to nine friends with the promise that you will receive great joy on the ninth day." It ended with a warning not to break the chain. The letters were not overtly threatening but they were very strange and were certainly ill-timed with what was already happening in the city.

After another night passed many African Americans in San Antonio "appealed to the sheriff and police departments for permits to carry weapons, and others, without such permits, have resorted to the use of firearms when aroused by strange noises in the dead of night," the *San Antonio Express* reported.

Three men were arrested for the murders, including two "Voodoo doctors" from Alabama, but, as the newspapers noted, "they denied any knowledge of the horrible butchery which has thrown seventeen separate and distinct kinds of scare into every negro in the city."

In the end, all three suspects were released. None of them could be linked to the murders. They just happened to be in the wrong place at the wrong time - with the wrong color of skin.

William and Carrie Burton, along with the two young children, were buried in City Cemetery No. 3, the same place where the Casaways had been buried the year before.

But before the funeral services for the Burtons could take place, the Axman had already struck again.

15. "WOMAN'S SCREAMS SAVED THREE LIVES"

HEMPSTEAD, TEXAS – APRIL 13, 1912

The Axman ended his spree with a double event.

Just one night after the murders of the Burton family in San Antonio, the Axman traveled east to the railroad town of Hempstead. Named for the town doctor in the 1850s, the town was home to three encampments of Confederate troops and a prisoner of war camp during the Civil War. By the early 1900s, it was gaining a reputation as the "watermelon capital of the world."

But the killer's victims achieved no notoriety in life and since few people know of their murders, little notoriety in death either.

Isaac "Ike" Burney was born into slavery in Georgia in 1855 and made his way to Texas at age 20, where he married Sylvia Johnson and had six children with her before her death in 1900. He eked out a living as a farm laborer and in 1912 was living a block east of the courthouse in Hempstead with his daughters - Cassie, age 20, and Alice Marshall, 30 - and Eva Jones and her two young boys.

In the early morning hours of April 13, he was attacked in his bed by the Axman, who was armed with either a small ax or a hatchet. Ike would not die immediately from his wounds. He lingered for three days before finally succumbing to his wounds and passing away.

The killer then slipped silently into an adjoining room, where Cassie, Alice, and Eva were sleeping. Alice was killed immediately when her skull was crushed. Cassie was also hit with the weapon, but before she could sustain fatal injuries Eva woke up and managed to escape with only defensive wounds to the hand that she raised to ward off the attack. She scrambled away, rolled off the bed, and then slid underneath it. She also began to scream, shrieking so violently that she scared off the Axman. Her screams not only saved her life but those of Cassie and her two sons, as well.

The killer fled the house, crashing out the door that he had presumably entered through and disappeared into the darkness. Later, police found rags on the ground about one block from the Burney house. They were tied in a way to suggest that the killer had wrapped them around his feet so that he could move silently through the house. If this was accurate, it explained how he had managed to enter so many homes without awakening any of his sleeping victims.

This was perhaps the strangest of the Axman's crimes, and perhaps it's fitting that it's officially the last. It was the first time that he had failed to kill everyone in the house, and the first time that he was seen as he made his escape. Eva was unable to describe him as anything other than a shape or shadow in the darkness, but the Axman had finally failed in his slaughter. Even the newspapers, so quick to endow the killer with almost supernatural powers, ran a headline that said, "Axe Man Bungled Job."

Could this be why the murders came to an end? Was his first failure enough to end the killings?

**The murders had become so much a part of public consciousness
that on Alice Marshall's death certificate, the coroner noted that
the cause of death was "Killed by the Axman"**

The Axman may have been interrupted in his slaughter,
but the papers were quick to point out that this had only been
the latest in a series of murders. The *Austin American-
Statesman* noted, "Crimes of a similar nature committed in
various sections of the state recently had caused abject fear
among the negroes of the town and locality, and today's crime
has completed the panic. So far, no clues that might lead to
the capture of the murderer have been found."

Nor would they be. The Axman may not have killed
everyone in the house, but he had killed. There was also no
question that he had become so entrenched in the public
consciousness that on Alice Marshall's death certificate the
cause of death is listed simply as "Killed by the Axeman."
Three days later, though, when Ike Burney died from his
wounds, the physician was a little more careful. Ike's death
was listed as "Struck on the head by the Axeman or some
unknown party."

Lawmen, convinced of a link between the murders, sent off detailed copies of their reports to other towns, asking for information on murders in their own communities, especially those that involved at least one person of mixed race and children.

Reporters for the *San Antonio Express* wrote:

Since the five bodies were found at the Burton home, men in the sheriff's department have been busy running down every available clue and the affair at Hempstead, seemingly similar to the one here, has redoubled their efforts. In an effort to determine whether all of these mysterious murders which have taken place at the dead of night in various towns in South Texas and Louisiana are not directed by intelligence, Sheriff Tobin dictated to his stenographer yesterday a full and complete account of the one here. Copies of this were sent to Glidden, Hempstead, Beaumont, and Lake Charles, La., with a request that the peace officers in those communities perform a like service for him. The information now at hand indicated that all of these crimes were similar, the distinguishing features being the families attacked contained at least one mulatto, that there were children in all cases, and in each instance some sharp instrument, such as a knife, was left sticking in the back of the victim.

It is the belief of those who have been working on the case here that the murders are due to the fanatical pseudo-religious teachings of a mysterious Church of the Sacrifice, whose ritual is reputed to be a queer jumble of Voodooism and biblical quotations. This organization also has many of the characteristics of a secret society and, if reports which have filtered into the police are true, those who are initiated into the mysteries guard them with zealous dread.

An old negro woman who conferred yesterday with Sheriff Tobin intimated that she knew something of the cult. She was wrinkled, decrepit and wore an old bandanna handkerchief about her head. Just who she was the sheriff declined to say, nor did he place much credence in her story. She explained that the words "blood of the lamb," used figuratively by Christians, has a more literal meaning in Voodooism, and gave this as a reason why children are killed.

The fact that the object of these murderous attacks are mulattoes is firmly established in the minds of the negroes and, while all members of that race here are more or less apprehensive, in those families where one or more is light-colored the fear is openly manifested. From midnight until dawn the mounted police are kept busy answering calls.

Fear of the Axman continued to run rampant through black communities. A black tramp who had recently arrived in town and was asking for food was feared to be the Axman. Suspicions about a recent addition to a black work gang caused the rest of the crew to refuse to work until the man was fired. When unsigned letters purporting to be from the Axman were found in several front yards in Austin, a delegation of black citizens met with the sheriff and asked for extra patrols in their neighborhood. They also created a petition to be sent to the governor requesting that he authorize a reward for the capture of the Axman.

In San Antonio, the newspaper reported that "The colored population secured all the guns they could find. Much excitement prevailed all night and many windows and doors were nailed up." In Bryan, fear of the Axman caused a panic one night that was only eased after a search of the entire neighborhood took place and nothing out of the ordinary was found. In Hearne, the presence of a letter "S," written in chalk, over the doors of some homes led many to believe that the Axman was marking the homes of his next victims. The situation was made worse by an unexplained electricity outage in town, putting police officers on heightened alert.

Although Jim Fields was still being held for the murders in Glidden at the time, the *San Antonio Express* reported on a "mass meeting of white citizens that was held at the courthouse to placate the negroes, to give them moral support and to offer any feasible protection that lies within their power against the Axman... The object of the meeting was stated by the chairman to be sympathy and protection of the colored people against the Axman." The meeting, which was about one-third white and two-thirds black, still managed to be racist, even with good intentions. However, it did adopt a resolution to request a suitable reward from the governor for the "apprehension, capture, and conviction of the Axman."

The fear being felt by the black population of the state did finally catch the attention of Governor Oscar Branch Colquitt, but there was little chance of catching the killer who had taken so many lives. The murders in Hempstead turned out to be the last of those committed by the Axman, but, of course, no one knew that at the time.

The murders may have ended, but the story of the Axman wasn't quite over yet.

18. THE "VOODOO LETTERS"

The governor understood the panic that was caused by the Axman, but it was the growing number of letters that people were receiving - allegedly sent by the Axman - that finally caused him to act. On April 19 he announced that the numerous threatening letters that were being received by people in various communities had caused him to offer a reward of $250 for the arrest and conviction of the person who was sending the letters.

But this did nothing to stop the letters that preyed on the fears of African Americans in Texas for months to come. Letters appeared in boxes, signed by "The Axman" or 'The Hatchetman." In Victoria, the authorities dismissed them as a joke, but families who received them weren't laughing. Most read, "We warn you, you half white, and all your family to leave town in ten days." In the town of Rockport, the receipt of several "Voodoo letters" led the black community to form a committee to "protect themselves against expected visits from the Axman." The committee also began meeting arriving trains to "note the arrival of strange negroes," the San Antonio Express reported. In Luling, slips of paper signed "Ax Man, Majority, and Gamge No. 25" were found under the doors of black residents. They came with warnings, "either vacate their buildings or leave town permanently." Many of the recipients heeded the warnings. Letters posted in Houston were sent to four black families in Columbus. Each of them included "pictures of skull and crossbones, a head with an ax sticking in it, and other devices with the words June 19."

The *Houston Post* carried a story about an ornate Axman letter that was received by a local family. "The envelope had been edged in black, making it a good imitation of mourning stationery, and in the center was a black coffin. Stamped on each corner with a rubber letter printing outfit was the following inscription:

Blood we want and Blood we Must have.

The letter inside the envelope read, "The Axman is in town and he is not a negro. This is a warning for you. Blood, blood, blood."

The letter sent the entire neighborhood into a panic. The police came to investigate and, in an effort to calm everyone down, dismissed the letter as "the work of some school children playing a joke at the expense of superstitious negroes." No one was reassured by this.

Another local family received a letter that wasn't nearly as decorated. It had a large skull and crossbones drawn crudely in the center and a large ax scrawled underneath. On the paper was written, "Look out, I am coming, you are next." It was signed "Ax Man." The police also dismissed this letter, writing it off as "the prank of some friend taking advantage of the woman's fear of the fiend."

The *Houston Post* reported another story of a cruel prank, but I have to confess, I'm a little skeptical about whether this actually happened. A porter on a return train from Beaumont went into the station master's office to change from his uniform into his street clothes but let out a loud cry and came running from the office in such a frantic state that he had to be stopped by several depot officials and a police officer. The cause of his fright was a potato that had been left on his suitcase that "had been carved to resemble a message from the ax man. It had a skull and crossbones, the porter's initials, and the sinister legend 'You Next' engraved thereon. It was signed the ax man." This prank caused so much amusement that someone took the potato and changed the initials to those of a cab driver and dropped it into his carriage. He was said to have been so frightened that he changed to working the day shift so that he could avoid any attention from the Axman.

Really? How big was this potato?

The *San Antonio Express* reported that in Elgin, the "axman fright had about subsided here when a negro man received a card reading thus: 'Harry, you are next from Axman, Mean Axman.'"

The Sheriff in San Marcos was given a letter that had been left as a clear threat to terrorize the African Americans in the community. The letter read:

I want to warn you that San Marcos is our next place and we are after all these stray niggers like yourself. If you are there when we make our raid we are mighty likely to get you. These stray niggers running over the country are the ones we are after. It will only be a few days before we get there. You can take notice if you don't think we mean business. Wait and see. You are not the only ones we are after in San Marcos. You had better lite out before we get there, which will only be a few days. We always send a letter ahead, in that way they don't believe it.

It was signed from the "Ax Committee," who was obviously not a group of scholars. They were taking advantage of the fear caused by the murders - and the letters that were circulating - to push their racist agendas.

Of course, not all whites were in favor of these tactics - far from it. A letter of support was sent to the *Alto Herald*, addressing the cruelty shown by the notes, but even when trying to help, the writer still managed to the drag in ingrained racism of the period:

During the last twelve months a large number of negroes have been brutally murdered by some person or persons in Texas and Louisiana. In every instance, men, women, and innocent little children have been brained as they sleep in their homes. The indications all point to the murderer being a negro, for an ax is the favorite weapon of the African. No matter whether he be black or white, I hope he will soon be apprehended, and will meet the fate he so richly deserves. Following these brutal murders, many negroes are receiving anonymous threatening letters, evidently written by some hellish white man, which have caused much unnecessary uneasiness among the blacks. Such an act is the height of brutality, and the writers themselves liable to a severe punishment if detected. They out to be hung.

An African American man named Elijah Branch wrote a letter to the *Houston Post,* suggesting that the post office should be investigating the "blackmail letters" for possible clues to the Axman's identity:

> *All efforts should be made to run down the "ax man" - the right one. It is possible in some cases for an ignorant negro to be caught, one who has not enough intelligence to exonerate himself, and yet he may be innocent of the crime.*
>
> *It ought to be determined by the officers of the law, first, whether this killing is inspired by a well organized society whose sole purpose is to intimidate the negro race or whether each case is independent of the other. In many cases persons have received blackmail letters which should become the property of the post office inspector, so he could examine same and see where mailed and what connection they bear to one another, if any. This, in my judgment, would be the only starting point for the post office department.*
>
> *I can only speak for my people. All of the law abiding negroes will unite with the peace officers in helping to run down these criminals, regardless as to who they are, and from the fact that they never have and never will be 'desirable citizens'.*

In Lafayette, Sheriff LaCoste even received an Axman letter. It wasn't threatening the lawman but instead was offering information to track down the killers, which the letter writer claimed to be part of. He was, he said, a member of the "105, who are banded together to kill negroes." He added that he was "disgusted with the ax murders and willing to confess his part in them." According to the letter, the band of killers chose the victims, and they were "marked in advance by a man who goes into towns and makes the necessary selections of victims, who are then dispatched by others." The authority cited in defense of the murders was the Sixth and Seventh Book of Moses. The writer also stated that he was not afraid of being caught by law enforcement officers but "is certain to have death meted out to him by his fellows."

Some of the attempts to frighten black residents went beyond mere letters. The appearance of what the *Plano Star-Courier* called "a peculiar looking man" was said have been wandering around the black neighborhoods in the city, trying gates, prying around, and starting a "panic among the local negroes, some of whom armed themselves and called on officers for protection, which, of course, they were assured they should have." The next day they found about a dozen signs hanging in the neighborhood - all with different wording - warning that the "ax man was coming."

Again, the police dismissed the warnings as a prank done by "boys who, knowing the superstitious nature of the negro, sought to frighten them. The better classes, who work and try to do right, have been assured they will not be hurt, and most of them went back to work Tuesday morning, although some of them were reluctant to do so."

And the final line of the article said it all - "Of course, the entire matter is regarded by the whites as a joke, and no trouble is anticipated by them."

It was difficult - perhaps even impossible - for most white residents to understand the terror that was being experienced by members of the black community. The murders that had been occurring for the past two years affected *only* African Americans, but that was not the main issue. No one knew that the murders had ended at this point. Not only did the Axman still remain a threat, but even if blacks knew the letters were pranks and were not coming from the Axman, they still had to deal with the very real threats that were implied in the letters themselves. In this era, blacks had more to fear from ruling class whites than they did from a mysterious killer. The murders had been random - in real life, they dealt with racist treatment every single day. According to the law, they were second-class citizens, largely at the mercy of the white police officers, business owners, and city officials. They were at risk of losing their livelihoods - and sometimes their lives - at the whim of any white person they encountered.

When the letters began arriving, I'm sure there were many African Americans who feared the Axman was sending them, but, for most, it was obvious that the letters were being sent by their white neighbors. Nearly every one of them threatened death or advised the recipient to "get out of town." The warnings were nothing new, but now they were allegedly coming from the sinister figure of the Axman. It was simpler to be frightened by a monster - a boogeyman lurking in the dark - than to be frightened by the racial threats that surrounded them every day.

The Axman became a meaningful figure in their lives, a legend on whom the worst things that happened could be blamed. The Axman had entered the African American folklore of the Deep South.

And he would never truly leave it.

Everyone remained on guard for the Axman, but having everyone armed to the teeth, staying up all night, and standing guard over their homes had its own issues - as Adam Bobinaux had found out in Beaumont when he accidentally killed his friend, Horace Alexander. For every man who tied a fishing line to his toe and attached the other to the doorknob so that he'd be awakened when it opened, there were 10 others who loaded shotguns and pistols and prepared to shoot at the slightest suspicion. In Houston, the newspapers said it was "not regarded as safe for a negro to move about after dark among people of his own race, as many of them announce an intention to shoot first and ask pedestrians as to their mission afterward." The amount of ammunition being sold - and reportedly stolen - was greater than it had been in years.

Dan Green of Yoakum was showing his wife how to use their shotgun - "in case the Axman put in an appearance while he was absent" - when it accidentally discharged both barrels and shot their daughter. An unnamed white man was followed using the trail of blood he left behind after trying to break into the home of a black woman named Mary Colter. He was shot by the woman's teenage son, who feared he was the Axman. A man named Willie Harris woke from a dream about the Axman and ran out of his house in terror, crashing through a glass door and sustaining cuts all over his body.

A Houston reporter wrote about a "vigilance committee" that had been organized to protect a black neighborhood. The men on watch were required to make five rounds of the neighborhood during their nine-hour watch and were fined $5 if they fell asleep on duty. One of the men on the committee told him that he had been on watch one night and saw someone walking around the house carrying what he thought was an ax. He grabbed his shotgun and ordered the figure to stop. Despite his fright, he warily approached the man with his gun ready, only to discover that what he thought was an ax was actually a shovel, being carried by the man who owned the house, who was walking in his sleep.

The unfortunate combination of panic and firearms caused two deaths in Smithville, Texas. Ernest Smothers, unable to sleep, got up and was walking around in the house, which was being guarded by Wes Duval who heard someone moving around in the darkness. He ran into the room and fired his shotgun at the figure he saw, killing Smothers instantly. A neighbor, Max Warren, heard the sound of gunfire, grabbed his own gun, and ran over to the Smothers house, but lost his nerve before he made it there. Another neighbor, Morris Sellers, also heard the gunshots, and when he saw Warren hurrying back home, mistook him for the fleeing Axman and shot him.

The *Brenham Daily Banner* announced, "One of the dreaded axe men has been caught at last, much to the gratification of many terrorized negroes who are in mortal fear of having their heads split open at night by the demon with the axe." The story was based on the arrest of Crawford Bray, a 42-year-old junkyard worker who had been arrested after terrorizing a black neighborhood. After drinking too much whiskey, Bray showed up at the home of his friend, Prince Judge, at 3:00 a.m. When Judge hesitated to let him in, Bray slurred, "I am the ax man! I want to get in the house, and if you don't open the door, I will blow up the place with dynamite!"

Bray did have an ax with him - probably why his friend wasn't inclined to let him into the house - so he slammed the door in his face. But Bray didn't stop there. He broke a window, climbed inside, and attacked Judge with the ax, slashing his arm. Everyone in the house was now awake and screaming. The women of the house were frantically trying to hide while the other men were confronting Bray, who was swinging his ax at them. By this time, the entire neighborhood was in an uproar. All they needed to hear was the word "ax," and they were convinced that killer had attacked again. The Reverend E.B. Evans gathered a group of armed men and they rushed to the Judge house. Bray tried to escape out the back door but was captured before he could leave. He was hauled away to police headquarters.

On the way to jail, Bray sobered up a bit and reportedly told the Chief of Detectives when he arrived, "Boss, I sure is sorry about this thing, and I wouldn't have had it happen for $5,000. I never is been in trouble and I never wants to be again." Bray was held for assault and murder but the charges against him were dropped a few months later - I assume when the authorities admitted that they had not arrested the Axman.

There was some good to come out of it, though. Reverend Evans used the incident as a teaching lesson, although I'm not sure if the lesson was to not pretend to be the Axman or to cut back on the alcohol.

Naturally, the white residents of Texas still managed to make the murders about themselves, even though the killer had claimed no white victims during his sprees. *The Temple Daily Telegram* printed an article that titled "Axman'll Get You If You Don't Watch Out," and it noted that the killer's presence had made itself known locally and "if you haven't seen or heard of him, most assuredly you have no communication with the colored population. The Axman is the most dreaded boy that has come to disturb the peaceful dreams of Senegambia (a region of West Africa) since the long-ago days when the "Paterole" or the 'Ku Klux' rode the lanes and by-ways."

The article was clearly meant for white readers who found the entire affair amusing, but there was also a somber note that stated, "it is to be considered that if a like epidemic of killing of families were to prevail with white folks as victims, there was be just as much fright as there is now among the darkies."

The all-night vigils waiting for the Axman were also an inconvenience to the whites who were dependent upon their black workers. *The Caucasian* (yes, a real newspaper) in Shreveport, Louisiana, reported that the "Axman's crimes have negroes of south Texas in state of terror at this time and in many instances have stopped work, making the labor problem a serious one." It was noted by the *San Patricio County News* that "domestic services in the town and field work in the county is seriously interfered with. It is almost a daily occurrence for a cook or yard man to report that they can not stay awake all night and work all day and that they will quit their positions to stay awake all night and sleep all day."

A local restaurant in Bryan decided to capitalize on the fear felt by blacks in their advertising. An ad in the *Bryan Daily Eagle and Pilot* advised, "When cookie is scared of the Axeman and don't put in an appearance or wife feels indisposed, call on the Owl Dairy Lunch!" Another read, "Say, did you find an 'S' on your door this morning? Well, don't be afraid of the Axeman, for that is the first letter in 'Stop at the Dairy Lunch!'"

I'll grudgingly admit that they were turning their lemons into lemonade.

The sensational stories about the terror being inflicted on African Americans in the region continued - and they kept selling papers. That was especially true when the stories focused on the possibility of Voodoo, folk magic, and all the racial undertones that went with them. Clementine Barnabet's stories fed much of the fascination that reporters seemed to have with the subject, and like the Voodoo article that had been published in El Paso earlier in the spring of 1912, reporters couldn't seem to stay away from it. Every article was incredibly racist - no surprise there - and filled with inaccurate information. But they really hadn't been written to "inform." They had been written to entertain.

An article that ran in the *San Antonio Express* is a perfect example of this:

These crimes have stirred up the negro population throughout the entire South, and it is not in San Antonio alone where members of this race are sitting up nights for fear of the mysterious "axman." Among many of the more ignorant ones there is a superstitious dread which intensifies this fear and which in turn may, and probably has, sent hundreds of them to local "witch doctors" for charms to keep away the executioner.

For years it has been known that despite the enlightenment of the Twentieth Century, a species of Voodooism has been kept alive in the "black belt" throughout the South. Few of the descendants of the slaves are more than four or five generations removed from barbarism and some even from cannibalism. Here and there an atavistic member of the race has handed down the weird practices of natives in Central Africa and in some instances improved on them. The result is that these "witch doctors" or "voodoos" as they are called, exercise a powerful influence over members of their race. They possess the "evil eye" and they "control the spirits" in such a way as to make them feared, and the average negro may laugh about it, but down in their hearts they can't shake off the dread with which they are possessed.

Moreover, these "witch doctors" do a thriving business, and if the truth be known, it isn't with members of their race alone. Many whites, just for fun, visit them, claiming, of course, that "it was just for the experience." Fortunes are told or possibly a "love potion" is given; in some cases, a charm is sold to ward off the "ha'nts." Practically every child in the South who had a negro mammy has at some time or another been to "de doctor's" house to have mystic words spoke or his head rubbed by the queer old darkey.

See what I mean?

Another frequent source for newspaper stories had to do with the many questionable measures that were being taken to try and ward off Axman attacks. Many believed that the Axman had somehow drugged the murdered families before he entered their homes, making it impossible for them to fight back. Earlier in the book, I mentioned that some families were placing wet towels at the bottom of their doors, trying to prevent the Axman from spraying sleeping gas inside. Others took it even further.

The *Temple Daily Telegram* reported, "The ways in which the precautions are taken are more amusing than effective. One favorite belief is that the Axeman in some way wafts chloroform into the sleeping room of his victims, thus enabling him to enter and kill all without arousing any. From somewhere, probably from a conjure doctor, it has been passed along that if water if placed in a vessel near the door some distance above the floor, the chloroform sill be taken up by the water instead of the fumes penetrating the room."

Rumors in Houston claimed that the Axman was using some sort of sleeping powder on the families, which could induce "a deep sleep from which they do not awaken before he has entered and brained them with an axe, his official weapon." There was, of course, a remedy to the sleeping powder being peddled by a "hoodoo man." Another "hoodoo man" remedy was a green ointment that could be rubbed on the head in large amounts but lost its power after nine hours and had to be applied again. One user complained that he "could not sleep on account of a fear that he would oversleep himself and fall victim to the axe man after the liniment had lost its power."

Strangers were still being seen as suspect in most communities, especially if they were believed to have any ties to Voodoo. "A strange and peculiar negro" named O.L. Escrow was reportedly going around Houston seeking a room to rent and writing down details about the houses he saw. He was reported to the police because several people believed he was the Axman, and he was arrested for vagrancy.

In Halletsville, a "negro fortune teller was compelled to leave town" after she warned the populace about an impending Axman attack. According to the *San Antonio Express*, a woman who arrived in Lockhart - "who from her dress and mysterious actions created the impression that she was in some manner connected with the much talked of Axman" - was arrested by the sheriff and given orders to leave town on the next train. In Belton, a "batty colored woman" appeared in town "arrayed in a royal purple skirt, was adorned with mammoth bows of red ribbon, wore a very large hat and black veil with a white cloth tied over her mouth, and her clothing was bejeweled with brass dresser drawer handles." She managed to cause a lot of excitement when she announced to everyone that she was "half-crazy and half-axman."

The Temple Daily Telegram carried a story about a Mrs. H. Williams who came to Bartlett "wearing false hair made from white people's hair and wearing quite a number of skirts with large pockets in them, full of various trinkets...

cheap jewelry, plate, knives and forks and other junk." She was arrested for vagrancy. She claimed that her husband was a faith healer and a fortune teller and while the police dismissed her as a harmless crank, the black community feared she was a "Voodoo priestess and that the trinkets and things found on her were to be used in the mystic ceremonies and rites of Voodooism." Of course, at that point, when Voodoo was being connected to the Axman, a crowd gathered at the jail and demanded that she be turned over to be hanged. The police officers in charge declined.

When a blind woman with dark glasses who claimed to be a "religious and educational lecturess" with alleged healing powers arrived in Victoria, her presence "created a general panic among the negroes of Victoria, who spoke of her as the axwoman," the *San Antonio Express* reported. "The more terror-stricken darkies threatened to kill her, and it took the combined efforts of the city marshal's and sheriff's departments to protect the woman." She was eventually allowed to stay in the home of a black deputy sheriff, who newspapers reported was "almost as alarmed as any other negro over the presence of the woman." He told her when he took her into his house that if she made a "crooked move," he would kill her.

The fear of the Axman continued into the summer, especially after several new attacks took place, but it seems the real Axman had vanished by this time. As far as I can tell, the last attack occurred in Hempstead, and after that, he simply disappeared. Where did he go? No one knows, but wherever it might have been, his mythology still lingered in Louisiana and Texas for the rest of 1912.

17. THE AXMAN ATTACKS THAT WEREN'T

In early June 1912, the black community in San Antonio was once again worked up into a frenzy of terror over what they believed was another thwarted attack by the Axman.

James Dashiell was a 40-year-old retired mailman who lived with his wife, Lula, and their three sons and a daughter. They had lived close to the Casaway family but had moved after they were murdered - to a new house just a couple of blocks away from where the Burton family had been murdered six weeks earlier.

Dashiell woke up in the middle of the night to find a man about to enter the side window of the house and seemed to have "what appeared to be an ax or a heavy club" in his hands. After the intruder fled it was discovered that he had cut the window screen and that, strangely, "red pepper was scattered about in the window and in the yard."

Was it the Axman? Maybe, or maybe not - it's impossible to know. Either way, no one was killed or even injured in the attempted break-in, so there's nothing to compare it with the earlier crimes.

But the community? As the newspaper reported, "Negroes of the neighborhood saw without reserve it was an occurrence sufficiently grave to again put them in fear for their lives." Protests followed, during which demands were made that African Americans be given the same rights as blacks to arm themselves against danger. Noting that "their votes have been sought to help place in office some of the men who are not now considering their rights," they planned to meet with state representatives and petition the governor to send Texas Rangers to the city to bring about a feeling of security.

The charged atmosphere of San Antonio was not about more than just the Axman. Because of appeals from the black community, Sheriff Tobin had already appointed several black deputies to serve in the city's African American neighborhoods. But problems began after four of the deputies were arrested by white city police officers for unlawfully carrying pistols. An unnamed official of the police department made a statement to the newspapers to justify the arrests:

Nearly two hundred negroes of the city have been deputized by Sheriff Tobin and in the belief that such authority gives them the required legal permission are carrying on their persons arms of various sorts, the greatest number having revolvers. We do not propose to place the lives of the police officers of the city in jeopardy through this indiscriminate 'toting' of firearms, and instructions have been issued to the force to make every effort to round up all persons unlawfully carrying arms.

Sheriff Tobin responded to the arrests - and the statement - with a message of his own. He had not appointed more than a dozen black deputies and that "the police department should view the arming of these negroes with alarm is rather absurd to my mind. The appointments were made solely because of the unrest created in the negro resident districts following the murders committed by the 'axman.' In these districts the protection afforded by the city police is practically null." He made it clear that each of the applicants had been thoroughly screened and that he did "not believe the police officers need fear any danger from those holding my appointments." Moreover, he filed a writ of habeas corpus to get his deputies released from jail.

M.B. Inman, one of the deputies who had been arrested, filed suit against the city marshal and three officers for false imprisonment asking for $20,000 in damages. In the suit, it stated that "he was arrested without legal warrant, confined in a 'vermin-infested cell room' and deprived of his liberty and denied bail." After he filed his suit he was finally released from jail on his own recognizance.

In late June, a Bexar County grand jury disagreed with Sheriff Tobin's appointments of the black deputies. The grand jury found that they had "been appointed in emergency, and no record was kept of such deputation. We have been advised that all such deputations have been recalled" and that "hereafter no deputation of any kind shall be issued without the proper course being pursued."

Sheriff Tobin didn't care and continued to stand by his men, even when campaigning for re-election to his office a month later. Speaking in front of the Alamo, he "defended himself in the matter of appointing negro deputies, explaining this action was taken after the appearance of the dreaded 'Axman' and that the negroes of the community were panic stricken."

And then he added, "I have no apology to make for this. I appointed some ten or fifteen of the leading negroes to patrol the streets in which they live, and should the same conditions arise again I would reappoint them. If you don't think this was right, don't vote for me, but I think those negroes were entitled to protection, and if I'm in a position to do so I'll give it to them."

Not only did Sheriff Tobin win re-election that year but he remained as sheriff until 1923 when he ran for Mayor. He won, and he continued to serve in that office until he died in 1927.

Sometimes, decency does prevail.

On August 16, the Dashiell home was broken into again. The newspaper described it as "what appears to be another visitation of the mysterious Axman... Undoubtedly the wielder of the ax had planned to wipe out the entire family, but his misdirected blows at the head of the woman failed to silence the first victim and her screams roused the other members of the family."

Lula Dashiell, who was sleeping next to her daughter, woke up to find a man with an ax standing over her. After a weak blow to her shoulder, she "quickly grabbed my child, all the while screaming as loudly as I could, when the ax struck me again on the ankle."

Awakened by her cries, her husband rushed in and fired several shots at the intruder, but each of them missed. The man fled the house and vanished into the darkness.

According to the police, however, this had not been an attack by the Axman. *The San Antonio Express* explained, "The officers were inclined to believe that the job was such a bunglesome one that the murderer who caused officers in this section to spend many sleepless nights would not be guilty of such an attempt." Officers went on to say that "the weapon used was not an ax, but the wound in the woman's arm was caused by a shot fired from a small-caliber pistol, while the bruise on the right ankle was a mere scratch, probably caused by a fall." It was not clear from the news report of the pistol shot had been fired by her husband.

Her screams awakened the entire neighborhood, and in the excitement, the belief that the Axman had visited the house began to spread.

On the morning of the attack, a newspaper story claiming that the Axman had returned again to the Dashiell home was printed in papers throughout the state, but the *San Antonio Express* was the only one that printed the correction to the story.

As for the Dashiell family, they left San Antonio after that. Axman or not, they had already moved once to avoid houses where the murders had taken place. They decided staying in San Antonio was not for them. They soon left Texas on a train bound for San Francisco and never returned to the state again.

There were other murders linked to the Axman that occurred that year but none of them really fit the pattern that had been established by the killer.

On June 11, a black woman named Plugan Reed who lived in Sulfur Springs was found with her head crushed in and an ax on the floor next to her body. Fear that the Axman had struck again began to spread, but her two-year-old daughter was found playing in the room with the corpse, making this murder quite different from Axman murders where the children were slaughtered along with their parents.

On July 6, a black livery stable employee in Port Arthur was found dead with his head smashed in after sleeping in the stable's office. The *Houston Post* called him "Another Axman's Victim," but there was nothing about the random killing that matched the earlier attacks. It did, however, give the paper an excuse to run an article on previous Axman murders and the running body count. They were doing what they could to keep the fading story alive.

Soon, the newspapers began speaking of the murders - and the panic that followed them - in the past tense. With no recent attacks in Texas and Louisiana the story turned cold, and the white community moved on. They hadn't lost any of their own, which made it easier for it to lose its relevance.

The black community had its own troubles that needed attention. The Axman would always be with them, but the sharp pang of fear felt when his name was mentioned eventually grew dull. People got on with their daily lives and soon worries turned to things other than a boogieman with an ax waiting to climb into their window at night - like jobs, food, housing, and poverty.

Today the murders are largely forgotten, but they shouldn't be. We shouldn't look at them with only a sense of morbid curiosity - we should also see them as a part of overlooked history and what this history says about how the past is viewed through the filter of race.

The Axman Murders remain an unsolved mystery. And that mystery goes beyond the question of who the Axman might have been and how he chose his victims. We need to ask ourselves how one of the largest murder sprees in American history - taking the lives of at least 45 men, women, and children - has been forgotten by a county that is so fascinated with murder.

Sadly, that mystery is easily solved by asking a simple question: what if the victims had been white?

AFTERWORD

Why did the Axman commit his crimes?

That's the nagging question that's left after reading about his crime spree through Louisiana and Texas. The answer is that we'll never know. There aren't enough records to detail the crimes in the way that we'd need to analyze his methods. There was no one checking for fingerprints or forensic evidence in the 1910s. We are only left with secondhand stories and newspaper articles, all of which can be questioned for their accuracy, especially when it came to white newspapers reporting on black crime victims in those days.

The motives of the Axman are hard to understand. They were obviously driven by hate and insanity, but a hatred for what? His own race? Was it because of what he considered the "impurity" of his race - an impurity created by the mulatto families that he seemed to target?

In 1972, William Ivy Hair published a paper about these murders and several other overlooked murders that occurred in the South during this period. He wrote:

In a society where blacks were liable to be mobbed for the slightest breach of racial etiquette, the centuries-old taboo against molesting whites was strong indeed. Even among violent blacks for whom the taboo posed no psychic obstacle, killing whites was, as a practical matter, a more perilous activity than killing Negroes. People of mixed ancestry, however, were classified by white society as being members of "the colored races." In effect, any discernible amount of Negro blood made one a Negro. To most whites, the murder of a mulatto family might be a regrettable incident, but was

*no more reason for an extensive manhunt than the murder of
a very black family.*

*It seems very reasonable to hypothesize that in the
mind of a violence-prone black of the early twentieth century,
the mulatto would make a convenient surrogate for the hated
white man. A light- skinned Negro, or a family with such
members, was the closest thing to a white person he could
destroy with relative impunity.*

Could he have been killing mixed-race families as a
substitute for the whites that he really wanted to kill? Perhaps,
it's an interesting theory.

Did it all have something to do with religion? I don't
believe it had anything to do with Voodoo, hoodoo, or any of
the other sensational religious mumbo-jumbo that the press
loved to talk about, but perhaps Sheriff Tobin was right when
he believed the Axman was driven to kill because he thought
"God told him to." He had been chosen, perhaps he believed, to
butcher the families that had allowed the race to mix.

But, if that were the case, wouldn't this make the
Axman more likely to be white than black, especially in that
era? It would seem likely, but again, there is no way for us to
know.

As many readers already know, the murders in
Louisiana and Texas from 1909-1912 were not the only ax
murders taking place at that time.

In New Orleans, Italian immigrants were being stalked
by their own Axeman, although most of those attacks took
place after these had ended. Those murders were connected to
a Mafia war of sorts between immigrant families, and while

they also were tainted by the supernatural, there was nothing to connect them with the Axman featured in these pages.

Mentioned briefly in the early pages of the book were the murders that occurred in the Midwest from 1911-1912, involving a killer I called "Billy the Axman" in my book about those murders called *Murdered in Their Beds*. Those murders were taking place at the same time as the murders in Louisiana and Texas, and the most famous set of killings took place in June 1912 in Villisca, Iowa.

Even though it's very easy for us to want to connect *all* ax murders to one another, there is no connection between what happened in Illinois, Colorado, Kansas, and Iowa, with what happened in Texas and Louisiana during the same period. The only similarities in the crimes seem to be that the two killers murdered families while they slept and likely traveled from town to town by rail. But that's where it ends.

Thousands of men worked for the railroads or rode them as transients in the early twentieth century, and newspapers of the time reports thousands and thousands of murders committed by an ax. It was a common tool in those days, in cities and on farms, and every house had one. It was a weapon of opportunity. If we tried to connect every ax murder to the sprees in the South and the Midwest, we'd have one man committing more murders than humanly possible.

I'll admit that I did toy with the idea that the Casaway family in San Antonio might have been the first of the Midwest Axman's crimes, but after further study, it became clear that the crimes were not related and that they were part of the Louisiana and Texas Axman's murders. It was an easy mistake to make - and I made it - but I honestly believe now that the Casaway murders have no connection to what happened in Villisca.

Or who knows? Maybe they do.

You see, that's the thing - we can have all the ideas, theories, and beliefs that we want to have, but there is no way to say that what we believe is the absolute truth. These murders are a mystery, as I already stated in the last chapter, but I think that what we do with that mystery is what makes the difference in how it's perceived.

I hope that I have not only provided you with an entertaining and spooky look at a string of murders from more than a century ago but that I have also given you something to think about when it comes to why the memories of those murders need to be memorialized.

Thanks for reading this book, and be sure to lock all the doors and windows before you go to bed tonight - you just never know who might be waiting to come in.

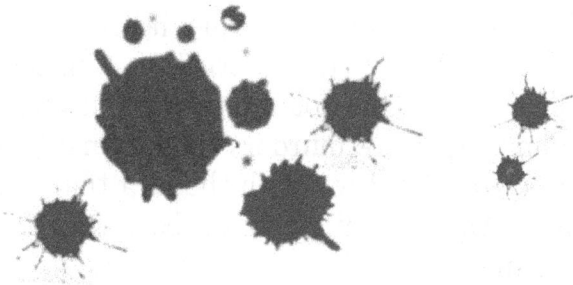

BIBLIOGRAPHY

Elliot, Todd C. - *Axes of Evil*, Waterville, OR, Trine Day, 2015

Hollandsworth, Skip - The Midnight Assassin, New York, NY, Henry Holt, 2015

Hudson, Marilyn A. - *When Death Rode the Rails*, Amazon Services, 2015

James, Bill with Rachel McCarthy James - *The Man from the Train*, New York, NY, Scribner, 2017

Kennedy, S. - *Jim Crow Guide: The Way It Was.* Boca Raton, FL: Florida Atlantic University Press, 1959/1990

Klingensmith, Beth H. - *The 1910s Ax Murders*, Unpublished; 2006

Swenson, Charles - "Waiting for the Axman: The Axeman Panic of 1912 in Texas," February 2019

Stein, Bill -- "The Glidden Ax Murder," Nesbitt Memorial Library Journal: A Journal of Colorado County History, Vol. 1, No. 10, p307-312

Taylor, Troy - *Murdered in Their Beds*, Jacksonville, IL, American Hauntings Ink, 2012/2016

Weber, Stephanie - *"The 'Voodoo' Murders of Clementine Barnabet"* Mental Floss, February 2017

Wells, Jeffrey - *The Atlanta Ripper*, Charleston, SC, History Press, 2011

Alto Herald
Amarillo Daily News
Austin American-Statesman
Bismark Daily Tribune
Bryan Daily Eagle and Pilot
Crowley Signal
Daily Signal (Crowley, Louisiana)
El Paso Herald
Houston Post
Lafayette Advertiser
Le Meschacebe (Lucy, Louisiana)
Monroe News-Star
New Iberia Enterprise and Independent Observer
Plano Star-Courier
Rice Belt Journal (Welsh, Louisiana)
San Antonio Express
San Patricio County News
Santa Fe New Mexican
St. Landry Clarion (Opelousas, Louisiana)
Temple Daily Telegram
The Caucasian (Shreveport, Louisiana)
The Times (Shreveport, Louisiana)
Times-Democrat (New Orleans, Louisiana)
Town Talk (Alexandria, Louisiana)

Weekly Advocate (Victoria, Texas)

Weekly Town Talk (Alexandria, Louisiana)

SPECIAL THANKS TO:

April Slaughter: Cover Design and Artwork
Becky Ray: Editing and Proofreading
Lisa Taylor Horton and Lux
Orrin Taylor
Rene Kruse
Rachael Horath
Elyse and Thomas Reihner
Bethany Horath
John Winterbauer
Kaylan Schardan
Maggie Walsh
Cody Beck
Becky Ray
Tom and Michelle Bonadurer
Susan Kelly and Amy Bouyear
And the entire crew of American Hauntings

ABOUT THE AUTHOR

Troy Taylor is the author of books on ghosts, hauntings, true crime, the unexplained, and the supernatural in America. He is also the founder of American Hauntings Ink, which offers books, ghost tours, events, and weekend excursions. He was born and raised in the Midwest and currently divides his time between Illinois and the far-flung reaches of America.

www.ingramcontent.com/pod-product-compliance
Lightning Source LLC
Chambersburg PA
CBHW071221090426
42736CB00014B/2926